A Different Paradigm in Music Education

A Different Paradigm in Music Education is a "let's consider some possibilities" book. Instead of a music methods book, it is a look at where the music education profession is and how music teachers might improve what it is we do. It is about change. It is about questioning the current music education paradigm, especially regarding its exclusive role as the only model. The intent is to help pre-service and in-service music educators consider new modes of pedagogical thought that will allow us to broaden our reach in schools and better help students develop as creative musicians across their lifespan.

The book includes an overview of several opportunities and course examples that would make music education more relevant and meaningful, especially for students that are not interested in our traditional performance offerings. The author wishes to stimulate discussions, with the goal for the music education profession to grow and mature.

David A. Williams is an Associate Professor of Music Education at the University of South Florida (USF). In addition to a variety of graduate classes, he teaches Foundations of Music Education and Progressive Music Methods to undergraduate music education students. He joined the faculty at USF in the fall of 1998, and he holds a Ph.D. in music education from Northwestern University. His research interests involve the use of learner-centered pedagogies and how these impact teaching and learning in music education.

Routledge New Directions in Music Education Series

Series Editor: Clint Randles

The **Routledge New Directions in Music Education Series** consists of concise monographs that attempt to bring more of the wide world of music, education, and society into the discourse in music education.

Eco-Literate Music Pedagogy
Daniel J. Shevock

The Music Profiles Learning Project
Let's Take This Outside
Radio Cremata, Gareth Dylan Smith, Joseph Michael Pignato, and Bryan Powell

A Different Paradigm in Music Education
Re-examining the Profession
David A. Williams

A Different Paradigm in Music Education

Re-examining the Profession

David A. Williams

Routledge
Taylor & Francis Group

NEW YORK AND LONDON

First published 2019
by Routledge
52 Vanderbilt Avenue, New York, NY 10017

and by Routledge
2 Park Square, Milton Park, Abingdon, Oxon, OX14 4RN

Routledge is an imprint of the Taylor & Francis Group, an informa business

© 2019 Taylor & Francis

Library of Congress Cataloging-in-Publication Data
Names: Williams, David Anson, 1958– author.
Title: A different paradigm in music education: re-examining the profession / David A. Williams.
Other titles: Routledge new directions in music education.
Description: New York ; London : Routledge, 2019. |
Series: Routledge new directions in music education series
Identifiers: LCCN 2018061603 | ISBN 9780367190088 (hardback) |
ISBN 9780429199806 (e-book)
Subjects: LCSH: Music–Instruction and study. | Curriculum change.
Classification: LCC MT1 .W57 2019 | DDC 780.71–dc23
LC record available at https://lccn.loc.gov/2018061603

ISBN: 978-0-367-19008-8 (hbk)
ISBN: 978-0-429-19980-6 (ebk)

Typeset in Times New Roman
by Newgen Publishing UK

Contents

Series Foreword

The Routledge New Directions in Music Education Series consists of concise monographs that attempt to bring more of the wide world of music, education, and society—and all of the conceptualizations and pragmatic implications that come with that world—into the discourse of music education. It is about discovering and uncovering big ideas for the profession, criticizing our long-held assumptions, suggesting new courses of action, and putting ideas into motion for the prosperity of future generations of music makers, teachers of music, researchers, scholars, and society.

Clint Randles, Series Editor

Preface

My musical background is band. I was, by every definition of the term, a band geek. This included being a clarinet player in middle school, high school, and as a college music education major. After successfully graduating with a four-year degree I became a high school band director, eventually returned to college for a Master's degree, and then I taught some more. I completed a Ph.D. program in music education and became a college level band director. I have seen the seven seas of band (say that quickly a few times!).

I lived the cyclical system we have developed in music education in order to propagate that what we do.

Band.

And choir and orchestra.

But two things changed me. Don't get me wrong, however. I still enjoy band.

And choir and orchestra.

But my music education world has forever been altered.

The first happened (started) in 2010. I formed an ensemble that played music using digital music instruments. We covered popular music songs and created our own original music. We did it all by ear. No notation. I had never experienced these things as a clarinet player in band. My bandmates, faculty and graduate students, all had previous popular music experience. They had covered popular music songs and created original music by ear without notation. But not me.

They were all really good at it.

I was really bad at it. I struggled. A lot.

But I got better. I was experiencing music differently. I started to hear music differently. This was an exhilarating musical adventure like I had never experienced in my life. I loved it.

I now have two basic emotions when I consider this experience. First, I am happy. I feel as if I'm much more of a musician than I ever was as a clarinet player or when I was doing band. Second, I am sad. I wish this experience had been introduced to me by my band directors a very long time ago. I feel blessed and cheated. Both at the same time.

This ensemble was, and is, a model of how a "learner-centered" pedagogy can function in music education. What I didn't know then, but I understand now, is this approach to teaching/learning situations in music makes the performers (the students) do the musical work. Because they do the work, they do the learning. And I learned (and grew musically) a lot.

Today, I involve undergraduate students in this ensemble. Students that are just like I was, with no previous experience covering popular music songs and creating original music by ear without notation.

The musical growth I'm observing in these students is pretty impressive. More, and faster, than the growth I saw when I was teaching band.

This is one reason why I wrote this book.

The second happened (started) just a couple of years ago when I took this "learner-centered" pedagogy into my non-performance-based music education classes. I stopped lecturing and started giving my students significant opportunities to "do the work." I sense that they grow more musically, and retain better, than when I (the teacher) did a lot of the work for them.

Guess what? This is also one reason why I wrote this book.

I wrote this book because the music education profession needs to consider expanding what we do and extending our reach. I wrote this book because we should examine different pedagogical approaches for what we do. I hope this book helps us do just that.

Introduction

In the text, *Questioning the Music Education Paradigm*, edited by Lee Bartel (2004), 23 authors "question the music education paradigm." Dr. Bartel asks, "But, what is it that they are questioning? What is a paradigm? Is there a music education paradigm? And what do these authors believe the music education paradigm to be?" He continues,

> A paradigm is a set of assumptions, concepts, values, and practices that constitutes a way of viewing reality for the community that shares them. In other words, a paradigm leads a group of people to agree "this is how it is and this is how it should be." What then is the music education paradigm? The music education paradigm may be best characterized by the rehearsal model – a teacher/conductor in front of a group of music makers controlling the starts and the stops, correctly diagnosing problems and effectively prescribing remedies to reach the goal of a flawless performance. Music education today is perhaps more teacher directed than any other aspect of schooling. The reason commonly given for this is sound: music making is noisy and, if all participants are not under central control, classrooms quickly degenerate into chaos. But music education also chooses the rehearsal model because our culture values music making and in the classical tradition the large ensemble is the most prestigious. Consequently we value highly the large symphony orchestras and they are driven by conductors and efficient rehearsal. Music teachers are trained in the tradition and literature and adopt the "model" as the one to aspire to. It becomes a pillar in our paradigm structure.[1]

The book you are holding is titled *A Different Paradigm in Music Education*. It is not meant as a music methods textbook. Rather, it is a "let's consider some possibilities" book. Obviously, ways of thinking will be introduced in this book that differ from the present "Paradigm." This book is about questioning the current music education paradigm, especially regarding its exclusive role as the only Paradigm. I am not suggesting we abandon our current paradigm. Instead, I am advocating that we adapt an *additional* paradigm – one that will allow us to broaden our reach in schools. I hope that reading this book will make you think. I hope it will make you consider new things. I hope, from time to time, that it makes you uneasy. I hope that it will stimulate discussions and arguments and agreements with your peers, your teachers, and with anyone involved with music education in the United States. I hope it will help the music education profession grow and mature.

Change. Why does this simple word represent such a difficult concept? Do you have any habits you have tried to change? Even if you were successful changing something, chances are you didn't have an easy time doing it. You are a special kind of person if change is easy for you, or if you enjoy making changes. Change is usually slow, frustrating, and painful, and most people would rather not even attempt change. Many attempts at change fall short of the goal. Change is just too burdensome. Those of us in the music education profession, as a group – we fall into this. Our profession would simply rather not change anything. We're pretty happy where we are. Oh sure, we would like it if we got more respect and funding, but these are somebody else's fault. Right? We're just misunderstood. There's nothing we could change that would affect the regard we receive from others, but it would be nice if we could get "them" to change what they do, so we could get more love. After all, music is really important and it makes you smarter … and nobody wants to change that (note: there is sarcasm dripping from this paragraph).

As it turns out, there are several obstacles that keep us from making change. Perhaps most importantly, change is usually associated with deeply ingrained habits in the ways we think and act. It's difficult to change something we've done for a very long time. Efforts to create change under these circumstances most often result in negative emotions such as fear, anger, and dissatisfaction. We find it hard to trust a change to the time-honored tradition. If we have a strong conviction about what we have been doing, it seems that change can only be for the worse. Since something new can't be as good as things are now, we go out of our way to make sure nothing changes. We also tend to surround ourselves with other people that are comfortable with the status quo, and together we feel secure with our traditional ways of doing things and we comfort each other as we go. The environment we create will not support change and in fact will most likely discourage change.

So here we are in music education. We are well into the twenty-first century and in the United States our profession is over 100 years strong. If ever there was a profession stuck in their ways, it is us. We are exceedingly happy with where we are. We feel good about what we do, and we are *terrified* of change. We've taught music in pretty much the same way since before most anyone can remember. There can't possibly be a better way to approach music in the schools since we obviously have had enough practice to know what is best. As mentioned before, any problems we are having are someone else's fault (I'm dripping again). The cuts to music teacher positions, the overwhelming number of secondary students that do not participate in school music classes, the inadequate funding, the lack of an actively musical society, our overall below-average status – these realities won't improve through change on our part (drip, drip). Things will only get better when "they" acknowledge us more appropriately and give us what we need, so we can do what we want to do. "They," by the way, include politicians, school boards, other teachers, principals, superintendents, legislatures, community members, students, parents, recording artists, and anyone else that might make our life better by changing their perspective.

Albert Einstein is credited with the quote "Insanity [is] doing the same thing over and over again and expecting different results."[2] I suggest this is exactly what we have been doing, and continue to do in music education. We insist on doing the same things, in the same ways, and somehow we expect our status in society will improve. The music education profession is not as healthy as it could be. We have tried for some time now to get better by hoping "they" will change to suit us. This strategy is not working, and it's time we tried a different approach.

This book is about change – change in the way *we* do things in music education. The change I will suggest does not mean we must abandon what we currently do, but I will encourage the profession to consider an additional paradigm with a very different approach to music teaching and learning. As uncomfortable as it might be, I suggest that our profession is at a tipping point where change is absolutely necessary.[3] I offer no apologies if you find yourself with emotions of fear and angst as you read this book. These might be natural reactions, especially if you have not considered changes to music education before. We have reached a point where we must move beyond our apprehension, and change aspects of what we do in order to attain a brighter future that is both meaningful and relevant for everyone within the society in which we live.

Notes

1 Part of an introduction to the text "What is the Music Education Paradigm" as found at www.bartelcameronassoc.com/music-education-paradigm.htm.
2 I found this on BrainyQuote: www.brainyquote.com/quotes/quotes/a/alberteins133991.html.

3 A "tipping point" has to do with an event that causes a balanced object to topple. After this point, the resulting change to the object cannot be stopped. To examine this concept applied to music education see John Kratus' "Music Education at the Tipping Point" in the November, 2007 *Music Educators Journal*.

1 Philosophic Thoughts and Questions

It is the one who does the work who does the learning.

(Doyle 2008)

If you are reading this book you probably are, or were, a music education major in college, and chances are very good that, when you were in high school, you were a member of a school band, choir, and/or orchestra. Chances are also good you not only participated, but excelled, in this activity. You may have been one of the most outstanding performers in your ensembles and were looked at as a leader by your peers. You probably helped the ensemble director by doing things like organizing and/ or handing out music, setting up for concerts, sorting uniforms, and moving equipment.

The reason I'm willing to guess these things are true about you is that they have been true for most college music education majors for a very long time. You might not think this is a big deal, but you would be wrong. It is a very big deal, and is a large part of why I wrote this book. I'll talk more about that later, but for now let me speculate about one more thing. I'm guessing you decided to be a music education major, in part, because you want to pass on to others the enjoyment, and triumphs, you experienced in high school music. You want to teach the next generation of students so they too can benefit from musical experiences in bands, choirs, and orchestras just like you did.

Pause for Reflection

Why do you think the above characteristics are true for the greater majority of music education majors in the United States? Why don't students with other musical backgrounds tend to major in music education? Why does this matter?

While there certainly isn't anything inherently wrong with wanting to pass on to others the joys and exhilarations that are a part of traditional school ensemble participation, one of my main goals for this book is to convince you that your role in music education needs to be something different – something bigger. Assuming your reasons for wanting to be a music teacher include what I just described, then I'm going to try and compel you to consider changing your mind.

More than anything else, this book is about change; change in the look and feel (and substance) of some aspects of K-12 music education. The thing is, change is hard. Most people feel uncomfortable making changes. Change can be threatening. This has been especially true in fields of education, and unusually true in music education. We will look closer at the history of our profession later, but for now, realise that what you probably experienced in high school music classes was, no doubt, very much the same as what your school music teachers experienced when they were in high school – and that was, in all likelihood, almost exactly what their teachers experienced when they were in high school. Change has been very difficult for our profession and our unwillingness to adapt to a changing world has cost us dearly.

In addition to having you consider change, the other main goal for this book is to get you to think deeply about the profession you want to enter. While you have, no doubt, seen the profession through the eyes of a student, there are certainly many aspects of the profession you have yet to experience. There is much to consider as you prepare to become a music teacher. It is likely you have developed some strong beliefs about the role of music in the schools. You may have a very good idea about the types of music with which you want to work, and how you want to teach. You can probably "see" yourself in your future position leading students to a fuller understanding of music.

Many students choose music education as a profession, in large part, because of the influence from a music teacher with which they have worked. Music education majors often report that they want to be like their high school or middle school ensemble director, teaching similar things in similar ways. This often comes out in music education classes (like the one you are in now perhaps) when a student reports to the class, "When I was in high school, we did _____ (fill in the blank)." Such reports could be about how a director handled unruly students, what types of music classes were offered, what styles of musics were performed, how part assignments were made, grading procedures, what fund raising products were sold, or what trips were taken. These reports are generally given with enthusiasm and a sense of pride. The general belief is that we know how things should be done.

An interesting phenomenon within education (as well as any of the social sciences) is that in *very* few cases are there right and wrong answers to questions. A lot of what we believe we "know" about education proves not to be as simple as we had imagined. What works well with one group of students might fail with a different group of students. No matter how successful your past musical experiences seemed, you must be careful not to assume that the way things were done was the "best" or the "right" way to do them. The ability to think deeply about the music education profession, and to consider alternatives, will be vital to your future success, and to the success of your future students.

I'll give you a personal example. I played clarinet in my high school band and I was pretty good. As it turned out, my best friend also played clarinet. He and I were always "challenging" each other to be "first chair." We had a pretty intense rivalry, and we both were motivated to practice a lot in order to improve our performance skills. Would you assume, as did I, that a competitive audition system, along with the ongoing challenge process, was the "right" thing to do? After all, it motivated the two of us to be the very best we could. So, I implemented an almost identical system when I began teaching instrumental music in secondary schools. I first auditioned all students and assigned them chair placements based on their performance, and I had a process whereby one student could challenge another student for "their" chair. I was sure this would create a competitive environment that would motivate students to practice and improve overall performance ability … and I was right … well, sort of.

There were a few students, mostly the more proficient performers, who seemed to thrive on the auditions and were motivated by challenging others and by being challenged. On the other hand, there was a fair percentage of students who were totally turned off by being forced to audition. Some of these students wouldn't participate, even if their grade was negatively affected by non-participation. I was amazed that I even had students drop out of the program in part because of their fear of competition. Finally, there was the vast majority of students to whom it didn't seem to matter one bit. I can't say that many of these students spent any additional time practicing in preparation for an audition or a challenge.

Were these same type of reactions occurring when I was a high school student? Wasn't every student like me, or is it possible I was so blinded by my own perspective that I didn't notice there were students who actually hated the idea of auditioning? You see, I had made a determination of what was "right" based on my experience. What I learned is that it is very difficult to determine what is best in a given situation, especially when I had only a very limited prior experience with that situation. I gradually changed my audition procedures over the course of my teaching experience to the point where I totally stopped auditioning students. Instead, I assigned parts to students making sure, that on any given concert program, all students had an opportunity to play different parts. For example, every clarinet player performed at least one "first clarinet" part, and they all played a "third" part. I found that, on average, students liked this far better than an audition system and it seemed that more students were practicing. I also found other methods by which I could provide additional motivation for those high achieving students that sought it.

I'm pretty sure I realized from the beginning that I didn't have all the answers (I still don't, by the way). What I had to learn, however, is that even in situations where I was sure I knew what was best, I didn't necessarily get it right. My recommendation is that you should question everything you do and everything you believe, especially in cases where you have become comfortable with something. You might ask yourself, "Why do we do it this way?," "Why do we need to do this?," "What if we did this instead?" etc.

As a way of getting started, let's take a look at a series of really important questions. I'm convinced it is not only vital that you have answers for these kinds of questions, but your answers should be well thought out after considering various alternative answers. I'm also convinced you can't be finished answering these questions in the few days during which your class will deal with this chapter. These are questions that *need* to haunt you for as long as you teach music ... they are that important!

What Is Music?

This is a great place to begin. You want to be a music teacher – so what is it you will be teaching? You might find it interesting to ask this question of various music faculty members where you attend school now, and several area K-12 music teachers. But don't stop there. Ask some local rock, hip-hop, and electronic musicians. Think you might get the same answers? If you can, you might also ask an Asian musician, or a Latin American musician. Can we actually define the term music? Is there one definition that might cover all that music can be? I'd bet you have already formed an idea of what music is for you – I'd only suggest you shouldn't assume your answer is the only "right" answer. And who knows, after looking at some alternatives you might change your mind!

There are some related questions, to which the possible answers have a great bearing on the question of what music is. For example, "Who makes music?" Are whale "songs" music? Do birds create music? Or is music something only humans do? Another example would be "At what point does something actually become music?" Are the noises and sounds babies make music? What about the beginner violin student making their first squeals and shrieks? Is the advanced trumpet player playing scales music? Yet one more example might be "On what can music be made?" Is a computer a musical instrument, or does it just make sounds "like" a "real" musical instrument? When used in a percussion ensemble is a car brake drum a musical instrument?

It is important that you seriously consider these types of questions. I hope you discuss these with your classmates. You should be ready not only with answers, but justifications for your answers, however, you should never assume that you "have it figured out." You need to remain open to other possibilities and new ideas.

Here are some of my impressions regarding the question, "What is music?" I don't have space here to go into much detail, but these should give you an idea of where I currently stand regarding the question "What is music?" See what you think ...

- I feel music is a human activity; something (both sounds and silence) that humans make, and something from which humans gain meaning.
- Creativity is an essential part of music making, so much so that I'm not convinced one is actually being musical when they have no creative input.
- Making music is not limited to just performance, but is inclusive of any of the ways humans interact with music creatively.
- Music (like other art forms) is a way of understanding (gaining meaning) that is different from, and not possible through, other pursuits.
- Music is meaningful for both individuals and groups of individuals (societies).
- All humans are capable of making music and all people are capable of obtaining meaning from music. Cognitive science suggests music is "hard wired" into humans at birth – that it is somehow essential to life – something people must do.[1]
- Making music, creatively and meaningfully, involves thought (cognition), feeling (subjectivity), and physical movement (psychomotor).
- The ability to make music (in all the ways possible) can be improved with study and practice, and the more a person understands about their music making, the more potential meaning that person can obtain from the experience.

If I had to sum up these thoughts in just a few words, I would suggest music has a lot to do with humans creatively interacting with sounds and silences in ways that are inherently meaningful and feelingful, both for themselves and others, and that the ability to "do" music, in all the many possible ways society provides, can be improved through education and practice. That really isn't a definition, but it certainly sums up the most important aspects of music (and music education) for me. What do you think? Have I included things that shouldn't be? Have I left out something really important? Am I way off base? Keep in mind my thinking has changed drastically since I first began teaching (right after the end of the Civil War), and I trust your thinking will change as you have more experiences with music and education.

A good number of individuals have done a lot of thinking and writing about what music is. There has certainly been quite a lot written on this subject by classical musicians (see Aaron Copland and Leonard Bernstein), not so classical musicians (see John Cage and Frank Zappa), and psychologists (see John Sloboda and Carl Seashore), just to name a few.[2]

Why Is Music Important?

Are you aware music has played a role in just about every society of which we know, in all of history? What's up with that? What is it about music that makes it so universal and so important to humans? My guess is SAT scores and math grades really have little to do with it. If music makes you generally smarter, why is it I've been a student of music for almost 50 years and I'm no smarter than the average person?

At least in countries that have mandatory education, like the United States, it is important to have a grounded understanding of why music is important for school-age students. This wouldn't be an issue if we had all the money we needed for schools, but that isn't the case – far from it. In times of limited resources, decisions have to be made regarding what will be taught in schools. We simply can't afford to do everything, and so those interested in music education (and education in all the arts for that matter) typically have to convince decision makers why funding should be spent (or continue to be spent) on music instruction.

For at least the last few decades, in order to justify the existence of music in the schools, our profession has concentrated on things external to music. Here are a few examples: 1) according to the College Board, students with multiple years of arts and music study scored higher on SAT tests;[3] 2) a Harris Interactive Study showed higher graduation and attendance rates in schools with music programs;[4] 3) "Tough Choices or Tough Times: The Report of the New Commission on the Skills of the American Workforce" indicates that mastery of the arts is just as closely correlated with high earnings as is technical skills (the report says this is a "fact").[5]

By the way, I learned all this by visiting the Advocacy sections found on The National Association for Music Education (NAfME) website.[6] These type of non-musical arguments have been the focus of music education advocacy for some time now. What kind of message are we sending people with these sorts of arguments? It appears that studying music in schools will make you better at taking standardized tests covering math and reading, make you go to school more often, give you a better chance of graduating from high school, and help you earn more. Can you think of some problems with these types of arguments? For example, is it possible that music study itself is not responsible for causing any of these outcomes? Is it possible high achieving students are drawn to music classes – students who, without the music study, would score well on standardized tests anyway, and be intrinsically motivated to attend school and graduate? Is it possible we might find similar results when looking at other activities like chess club, driver's education, culinary classes, oceanography, etc., so that eliminating music classes wouldn't really matter since students could still gain such advantages in other ways?

While these arguments may be helpful in some situations, I suggest we have to do better. Is there something humans might obtain from music study that they can't get from doing other activities? Is there some benefit uniquely derived from music study; some benefit that is also essential for all people? Is there some benefit from music study that would be profoundly missed if young people were denied it in school? If our profession is truly "basic," as we like to proclaim, and if music study is important for all students, as we typically suggest, then we must advocate for music in the schools based on rationales that go beyond those suggesting our value is built on the importance of other disciplines.

As with the question, "What is music?," there has been a lot written regarding the importance of music and music education. At the very least, it would be well worth your time to look into some of the work by two music education philosophers, namely Bennett Reimer (2003) and David Elliot (1995). Reimer is most closely associated with the aesthetic education movement that dominated music education philosophy beginning in the 1960s. His book, *A Philosophy of Music Education*, now in its third edition, is considered by many to be a salient piece of music education literature. Reimer provides the following description of aesthetic education that encapsulates much of his philosophy:

> Aesthetic education in music attempts to enhance learnings related to the distinctive capacity of musical sounds (as various cultures construe what these consist of) to create and share meanings only sounds structured to do so can yield. Creating such meanings, and partaking of them, requires an amalgam of mind, body and feeling. Musical meanings incorporate within them a variety of individual/cultural meanings transformed by musical sounds. Gaining its special meanings requires direct experience with music

in any of the ways cultures provide, supported by skills, knowledge, understandings, and sensitivities education can cultivate.

(Reimer 2003, p. 11)

For Reimer, significance in music involves both the capacity of music to embody human feeling as sound and the ability of humans to share meaning through music. Reimer believes that the human condition is uniquely enhanced by involvements in music listening, performance, composition, and improvisation and this enhancement is capable of being heightened through education.

Elliott's philosophic views are put forth in his 1995 *Music Matters: A New Philosophy of Music Education*, and are identified as praxialism. While Reimer talks of music as a noun, Elliott sees it as a verb and uses the term "musicing," indicating that music is something humans do. Elliott describes the basic components of praxialism as follows:

> The praxial philosophy holds that music has many important values. Self-growth and self-knowledge – and the unique emotional experience of musical enjoyment that accompanies these – are among the most important values of music and music education ... In addition to these values, musicing and listening extend the range of people's expressive and impressive powers by providing us with opportunities to formulate musical expressions of emotions, musical representations of people, places and things, and musical expressions of cultural-ideological meanings.
>
> (Elliott 1995, p. 10)

Both Elliott and Reimer traded shots, pitting their two philosophic stances against each other. In his third edition of *A Philosophy of Music Education*, while still critical of Elliott, Reimer does present several synergistic proposals. While the tenets of aesthetic education and praxialism do indeed have real differences, there is much the two views have in common – and these commonalities are well worth your consideration. These include:

- The importance of music education depends on the importance of music within a culture.
- Being musical involves complex cognitive and affective processes that are meaningful to humans.
- Listening intelligently to music is meaningful affectively, interpretively, structurally, expressively, representationally, socially, and personally.
- Music engages and challenges our powers of consciousness (including attention, cognition, emotion, feeling, and memory).

- Self-growth and self-knowledge, regarding feeling, thinking, knowing, valuing, and evaluating, develop alongside musicianship.
- Musical expression and creativity provide opportunities for the creation and sharing of emotional meanings that are uniquely afforded by musical involvements.
- Musical involvements are necessary (accessible and applicable) for all students.
- Musical involvements in schools should involve a variety of styles including popular genres and musics from other cultures.

Pause for Reflection

What is the value of philosophy for the music education profession? What is the value of a philosophy of music education for you personally?

In addition to Reimer and Elliott, there are several prominent music education philosophers who have recently added important considerations to the discussion concerning what music is and why music education is important. Among these are Wayne D. Bowman, Estelle R. Jorgensen, Thomas A. Regelski, Christopher Small, and Paul G. Woodford.[7] Consideration of this work is beyond the scope of this text but it would make for a worthwhile class project if small groups of students looked into individual writers!

There are some other questions we should address when talking about the importance of music. For example, does it matter what styles of music are studied? Do students receive the same types of benefits from studying popular music styles as they would from more traditional Western European classical musics? Are the same type of benefits realized from working with unfamiliar musics from other cultures? Is there some combination of different styles of musics that would be even more beneficial? Furthermore, does the type of musical involvement matter? Do students get the same benefits from one-on-one study as they get from chamber groups, as they get from large ensembles? Would it be better if a music class included all these settings, or is it more advantageous to concentrate on one or two? What about the nature of instruction? Are the same types of benefits realized from teacher-centered instruction (where the teacher is the sage on the stage) and learner-centered instruction (where the teacher acts as a guide on the side)? Are formal types of learning environments more beneficial than informal? It probably isn't sufficient to merely suggest any music study is good for students. This is simply too broad a statement. We must have a better understanding of the most beneficial types of music instruction for different age students and different types of students. I will make suggestions later in this book regarding characteristics of music instruction that could improve music education in schools and would advantage students with lifelong musical skills, but for now I would advise that you seriously consider why music is important to people and how we might go about providing the best environments for music learning.

What Is It a Musician Can Do?

Whenever I pose this question to students, the first answer is usually – perform on an instrument. A musician is someone who performs music, especially on traditional orchestral instruments, right? Performance ability on a musical instrument is normally seen as vital in order for one to be considered a musician. How accurate is this claim? Are there aspects of real musicianship that can be developed in ways apart from performance, or is it really all about performing?

I've got this friend who has an amazing vinyl record collection (yes, vinyl!). You may have heard about these … we used to call them records. He has thousands of recordings, mostly classical. He can tell you about every nuance in any Beethoven symphony or string quartet. He knows this music – he understands this music, like most of us never will. He finds meaning in this music – serious meaning! However, he plays no musical instrument – never has. Is he a musician?

What about someone who writes music for others to perform? What about a music theorist or historian or therapist? Are these people not "doing" music? I suggest that our culture makes available several ways in which people can be musical, and that performance is not necessarily required. If, however, performance ability is a requirement for one to be "musical," then at what point does one become a musician? On the first day of beginning band, when making his first sounds on a trumpet, is the student a musician? Does he have to know all his major scales before he can be considered a musician? Does he need to know how to read traditional music notation? Does he first need to receive a superior rating playing Hayden's trumpet concerto at a solo festival? Is there a point at which a performer moves from being "not a musician" to being "a musician?"

This is a very important issue for music educators. By looking at traditional music education offerings in schools one could assume a musician is a performer that sings, or plays a certain type of instrument (most notably, a Western European orchestral instrument) primarily in large groups. This is a pretty limited view of musicianship. We tend to further limit the definition even more by giving increased attention to the best performers through such things as chair placements, honors ensembles (All-County and All-State), and awards. By perpetuating a limited view of what it is to be a musician we have effectively cut ourselves off from a good number of students who do not aspire to be musical in this particular way, yet love music and want to become more musical.

In the cartoon strip "Funky Winkerbean," the high school band director, Harry Dinkle, once said that there are two types of high school students – band students and juvenile delinquents. The thing that makes sarcasm so funny is that many people (like those of us involved in formal music education) think it's not sarcastic at all!

An important, and closely related, question has to do with the development of musicianship. How is it that someone becomes a musician? Is it necessary to "go to school" or to "study" to become a musician? Is it something that someone can do sitting in their bedroom by themselves, or with a group of friends in the garage? What is it, in schools, that we might offer students interested in developing musicianship skills that they can't get from watching teaching videos on the internet?

I worry we have become so accustomed to the status quo of traditional music education that we feel as if we "have it right" – and that we presently offer students the best route, perhaps the only true path, to becoming a musician. It is easy to be deceived by a sense of security when we use blinders to shield our vision from other possibilities. I suggest this is exactly what we have been doing. Our successes with one particular type of musicianship have contributed to our being blind to other possibilities. Keep in mind that one of my main goals for this book is to convince you that your role in music education needs to be something bigger than the status quo.

What Should Be the Goals of Music Education?

I've been in the music education profession for a long time now, and I've sat in a good many high school band, choir, and string classrooms as a student, teacher, clinician, recruiter, performer, conductor, student teacher supervisor, parent, and guest. Often, in the course of visits, I will be talking with the music teachers at a school and learn that "X" number of music students from last year's graduating class are now music majors in college. Such statements are most often made with a sense of honor and pride. Obviously, there is nothing inherently wrong with this. It would be a real problem if there were no students who were interested in music education as a profession after their high school participation, however, it's interesting so many high school directors would think these particular data are so important. Along the same lines, I often hear elementary school music teachers explaining how their music programs prepare students for ensemble participation at middle schools, and middle school teachers who consider their classes as "feeders" for high school programs. I am left to wonder how important a goal all of this is. While preparing students for another level of musical experience might be necessary in some ways, our fascination with this particular goal is intriguing. An awful lot of students will not have aspirations for a next level and they will never attain this goal. Do you think they ever notice how much we dwell on it? Perhaps the main goals of music education should involve things that are attainable in whatever level a student presently resides?

What goals do you have in mind for your future teaching? Do you want to direct a big marching band, or a swing choir that performs 40 programs a year in the community, or a professional sounding orchestra? Do you want students to understand music history and culture? Do you think every student should understand music notation? These might be worthy goals. Are you interested in producing a program in which students have fun and where they feel safe and welcome? Do you want to produce professional musicians? Do you see your program having competitive aspects that win competitions? I've known teachers whose main goal was to get through another day of school; others who believed their classes provided a break from the academic rigors of other classes. There are many potential goals, including several I doubt you have even considered.

Of all the conceivable goals for music education, there probably are a few that should rank as the most significant. Some of these, I suggest, should be closely related to your answers of previous questions like, "What is music?," "Why is music important?," and "What is it a musician can do?" An appreciation for the importance of these will go a long way in helping you formulate goals that are essential for your future students. A goal that is of the utmost importance for me has to do with helping students develop lifelong musicianship skills. I want my students (all of them) to gain the capacity to creatively interact with musical materials, and increasingly find fulfillment and significance (meaning) from their musical activities, both independently and with others, for as long as they choose. This goal is closely related to my beliefs about music (made by humans), why it's important (inherently meaningful), and what it means to be a musician (creative).

By the way, I'm sorry this statement about my goal is so wordy. I wish I could express the things I feel about music in fewer words, but as I'm sure you've figured out already, there is something about music that is hard to describe using only words. But that doesn't mean it isn't important that we continue to try – in fact, it's possible the future of our profession might depend on it.

Why Does "Doing Music" Look So Different Outside the Schools?

Do you know the term "an elephant in the room?" It usually refers to something that is obvious, but which people choose to ignore. Typically, the decision to ignore a situation is predicated on fear or apprehension. I think we have a few elephants in our profession. One involves the differences between what we do musically in schools and what our students do musically outside of school. There is generally little (if any) connection between our traditional school music offerings and the musics of our culture. This is especially true if we look at the musics that dominate popular culture and/or youth culture. For a very long time we (the music education profession) have isolated ourselves musically from the culture that students experience outside of school. We have made attempts at including pop songs with different ensembles, but often these attempts are far from authentic, and as a result are less than genuine. While there are certainly exceptions, they are too few and far between. It's troubling that while the music education profession tends to ignore this elephant, school students are clearly aware of it.

At the University where I work we have a terrific marching band program that includes a 30-member Ceremonial Band. I think of this group as a Special Forces unit. They are elite players, who are ready on almost a moment's notice, and they perform for a wide variety of events both on and off campus, where they play a good number of popular music arrangements. And they are really good! Recently I observed a crowd of students listening to the Ceremonial Band play at an event on campus. The event was a showcase for arts on campus and included some theater, dance, visual art, and various musical ensembles. The biggest crowd was attracted by the Ceremonial Band (not counting the host of free food tables that was the real attraction for most in attendance). While I watched the students enjoying the Ceremonial Band it struck me that, while they were obviously entertained by the music, their responses were very different than what you might expect when students of this age range attend a typical live music concert. While the Ceremonial Band was playing arrangements of music that were hot off the radio, and the students present were enjoying it, it still wasn't the same as the "real" thing as represented in popular culture. Here was our best attempt at reaching students with music from their culture and it was falling short. The experience made me interested in taking a look at the playlists on these student's music players, to see how many of them had any marching band arrangements ... I bet I wouldn't have found many. Even though we, in the profession, count this as using popular music in the classroom, it is still "school music" to most students.

Why should we care about how music is practiced by the society in which we live? Why would we want to do in the classroom what students already do without us? Isn't it our obligation to expose students to the Western European canon? Your answers to many of the previous questions I posed, again, are closely related to this issue. The goals you set for your program and students will help inform your views on whether you are concerned with representing youth culture in your classroom. For example, if the most important goal for you is that your ensembles achieve high ratings and rankings at festivals and contests then it is not likely you would be interested in involving study of popular musics in your teaching.

For years now there have been all kinds of claims concerning the percent of students that enroll in secondary school music classes. I've heard numbers ranging from 10% to 30%. I have seen actual Department of Education data from my home state of Florida (FDOE) showing that the percent of high school students enrolled in music classes across the state dropped from 16% to 11% during the 20 years between 1985 and 2005.[8] Both these numbers, and the trend, are alarming. By the way, these numbers include *all* music classes and not just traditional ensembles. Additional FDOE data from 2017 show that less than 10% of high school students enrolled in band, choir, and orchestra classes.

While this is only for one state (however, the third largest state in population), I would think music programs in many other states are in a similar situation. A recent study by Elpus and Abril (2011) indicated that across the United States, 21% of seniors in the class of 2004 took part in school music classes. These data represented a 10% decline in music participation compared to a similar study completed by Stewart (1991).

I know what you may be thinking. There are a lot of reasons for the low numbers. Academically advanced students may opt for more Advanced Placement courses, and academically challenged students may be forced into remedial courses, leaving both populations with fewer elective opportunities to include music. Then there are scheduling conflicts, uncooperative counselors, block schedules, students with too many competing interests or the need to work, and the list of excuses goes on. If anything, I would suggest we have become quite proficient at making excuses by pointing fingers at things we can't control. The cause of the problem is certainly someone else's fault – right? While there are issues we cannot control, there is more to the story.

I doubt you know much about the old cartoon strip *Pogo*, but there is one scene where the title character is surveying environmental damage and he says, "We have met the enemy, and he is us." Let me suggest that this characterizes the music education profession's situation in the schools. We are just as much to blame, if not more so, for the low numbers of students that elect to take music classes in secondary schools. Wayne Bowman (2009) eloquently puts it this way:

> Music education has lost touch with the diversity and the fluidity of its subjects, and their fundamental nature as human practices … We have embraced particular modes of musical engagement (performance, for instance) as though they exhausted the range of educationally useful musical action. We have sought to universalize instructional systems and strategies that are effective only under certain conditions. This naïve faith in one true way of being musical and of implementing curriculum is rooted in an understandable human need for confidence and security. But it is not well suited (whatever its therapeutic value) to the musical needs of students in a diverse and changing society.
>
> (Bowman 2009, pp. 8–9)

We will look further into this issue later in the book, but it certainly seems our reluctance to conceive of music education as anything other than traditional large group performance is costing us dearly. If, as a profession, we feel music study is essential for all students, then we must do something to seriously address the differences between music study in schools and the way students use their musical skills when they leave school.

Pause for Reflection

Do you feel the music education profession has "lost touch with the diversity and the fluidity of its subjects, and their fundamental nature as human practices?" Why or why not? Had you ever considered this issue before now? Why might that be important?

What Are the Challenges Ahead for Music Education?

Are we content with the present condition of the music education profession? If so, then perhaps the previous questions aren't that important. If you feel the main goal for K-12 music education is to help identify and train the future classical musicians and teachers, then you are probably pretty happy with the way things are. In fact, we probably don't need 10% of secondary school students in music programs to manage this goal. However, if we have higher aspirations for our profession, I would suggest the previous questions are of great significance, and

I believe they lead to more questions. Are our present offerings relevant for today's students? How do we reach the students who aren't interested in our traditional offerings? How do we attract a diverse range of students that more closely represents the ethnic and racial makeup of our schools? How do we deal with new music technologies? How should we handle multicultural and world musics? How do we increase the number of students that continue making music after high school? How do we go about having a greater impact on our nation's musical culture? How do we prepare pre-service teachers, and retrain in-service teachers for a changing future? There are certainly challenges ahead for our profession – perhaps more so than at any time in our past. Are you prepared to consider the options as we move forward?

Pause for Reflection

That's quite a lot of new questions. For which of these do you think there are easy answers? Which are more essential than the others? What answers do you have for any of these questions?

I'm guessing by now you understand why these questions are so important for the music education profession. A profession, by the way, of which you are the future. I assume you noticed that instead of offering many answers to the questions above, I ended up posing even more questions. That is the problem with education, which is a branch of the social sciences. There are always more questions than there are answers, and the answers that seem to be correct today may not be so "right" next year. Teaching is not an easy job. It can, however, be very rewarding. It can also be quite frustrating. Too many beginner teachers quickly become discontented and end up leaving the profession after teaching only a year or two. If you would like to avoid having this happen to you, I would suggest you seriously begin thinking about and reflecting on the questions that have been presented in this chapter. While this won't guarantee success, it will certainly help you be better prepared for the realities of our profession.

Notes

1   Howard Gardner's work is an excellent place to start, and his 1983 book, *Frames of Mind: The Theory of Multiple Intelligence* is a must read for music teachers.
2   In addition to their distinguished accomplishments as composers, Aaron Copland and Leonard Bernstein were both great thinkers and writers about

music. Copland's *Music and Imagination: The Charles Eliot Norton Lectures*, and Bernstein's *The Joy of Music* provide an insight to their thinking. John Cage and Frank Zappa are musicians who came from very different musical backgrounds and also offer interesting insight into the nature of music. Cage's *Silence* and Zappa's *The Real Frank Zappa* are interesting reading. Carl Seashore and John Sloboda present different views of music from the eye of the psychologist. Seashore's landmark *Psychology of Music* and Sloboda's *The Musical Mind* are excellent reads.

3 See the "CollegeBoard SAT Total Group Profile Report, 2006 College-Bound Seniors" (page 9). Similar results were found from reports in other years as well.

4 Harris Interactive Report, "Understanding the Linkages Between Music Education and Educational Outcomes," July 6, 2006.

5 "Tough Choices or Tough Times: The Report of the New Commission on the Skills of the American Workforce," 2007. The Executive Summary is available online as a pdf file. The full report was published by Jossey-Bass, a Wiley Imprint. The Commission's Website can be found at www.skillscommission.org.

6 https://nafme.org/my-classroom/music-achievement-council-resources-educators/.

7 See Wayne D. Bowman, *Philosophical Perspectives on Music* (1998), published by Oxford University Press; Estelle R. Jorgensen, *In Search of Music Education* (1997), published by University of Illinois Press, and *Transforming Music Education* (2003), published by Indiana University Press; Thomas A. Regelski, *Teaching General Music in Grades 4–8: A Musicianship Approach* (2004), published by Oxford University Press; Christopher Small, *Musicking: The Meanings of Performing and Listening* (1998), published by Wesleyan University Press; Paul G. Woodford, *Democracy and Music Education: Liberalism, Ethics, and the Politics of Practice* (2005), published by Indiana University Press.

8 The Florida K-20 Education Data Warehouse (EDW) is part of the Florida Department of Education and provides data related to Florida's Kindergarten through University education. According to the 2010 census, Florida had the fourth largest population in the U.S., but since then it is estimated to have eclipsed New York with the third largest (https://en.wikipedia.org/wiki/List_of_U.S._states_and_territories_by_population).

Readings and References

Bernstein, L. (2004). *The Joy of Music*. Pompton Plains, NJ: Amadeus Press.

Bowman, W. D. (2009). No one true way: Music education without redemptive truth. In Regelski, T. A. and Gates, J. T. (eds.), *Music Education for Changing Times: Guiding Visions for Practice*; Landscapes: the Arts, Aesthetics, and Education series, Volume 7. New York: Springer.

Cage, J. (1973). *Silence*. Middletown, CT: Wesleyan University Press.

Copland, A. (1980). *Music and Imagination: The Charles Eliot Norton Lectures*. Cambridge, MA: Harvard University Press.

Doyle, T. (2008). *Helping Students Learn in a Learner-Centered Environment: A Guide to Facilitating Learning in Higher Education*. Sterling, VA: Stylus Pub.

Elliott, D. J. (1995). *Music Matters: A New Philosophy of Music Education.* New York: Oxford University Press.

Elpus, K. and Abril, C. R. (2011). High school music ensemble students in the United States: A demographic profile. *Journal of Research in Music Education* 59(2): 128–145.

Gardner, H. E. (1983). *Frames of Mind: The Theory of Multiple Intelligences.* New York: Basic Books.

Reimer, B. (2003). *A Philosophy of Music Education: Advancing the Vision*, 3rd ed. Upper Saddle River, NJ: Pearson.

Seashore, C. E. (1967). *Psychology of Music.* Mineola, NY: Courier Dover Publications.

Sloboda, J. A. (1999). *The Musical Mind.* New York: Oxford University Press.

Stewart, C. (1991). Who takes music? Investigating access to high school music as a function of social and school factors. Doctoral dissertation, University of Michigan.

Zappa, F. (1990). *The Real Frank Zappa Book.* New York: Simon and Schuster.

2 History and Traditions

In order to better understand where we are, and where we want to go, it's a good idea to ground ourselves in where we came from and how we got here. I will frame this look at history beginning in the mid-1700s. This leaves out extraordinary musical traditions that were well established here by the time explorers began settling, however, compared to the European impact, these native musical practices have had little influence on the daily music practice and study in the United States. For those interested in a much deeper examination of music history in the United States, see *A History of American Music Education*, by Michael Mark and Charles Gary. It is an outstanding historical source beginning with influences from the Hebrews of the Old Testament. Also, Edward Bailey Birge's *History of Public School Music in the United States*, which was first published in 1928, is a fascinating look at music practice from almost a century ago (while a lot of what we call history was actually happening).

As Europeans began settlements in what was to become the United States, they brought musical and educational traditions with them. Singing, especially hymns and psalms, was vital for the early settlers, particularly in the Northern colonies and states. However, by the 1720s the quality of sacred singing had diminished greatly. There were, no doubt, several reasons why musical skills declined in the New World, but ventures to improve the situation influenced music education for the next hundred years. The most important of these was probably the introduction of "the singing school" as these schools laid the foundation for formal music education in America.

Singing Schools

A singing school consisted of a music teacher, or singing master, that held classes in towns and cities where people wanted to learn how to sing and read notation. The notation used was not always what we consider traditional notation today, but rather it often was one of many variations of notation systems based on solemnization (solfège) syllables and/or shape notes. The basic intent for using these systems was to simplify music reading. Normally, a music teacher would travel to a town and rent a classroom, church, home, or other meeting place and they would advertise their services in whatever ways were available to them. Students (of all ages!) would pay the singing master directly, sometimes using a barter system. Classes would often meet in the evenings, from one to several times a week. Normally a teacher would stay in one location for a few weeks to several months before moving onto another town to set up school there. A concert/recital would often be held, at the conclusion of instruction, where students would perform, sometimes with a local minister providing a sermon. The music teacher would also sell merchandise including tune books, often composed by the teacher himself. The first singing schools used sacred music almost exclusively, but in time, secular music began to be added as well.

In addition to musical aspects, the singing schools provided a social experience for students. They were popular in part because they provided a social gathering opportunity for people with similar interests. While the singing school movement had its roots in the New England colonies, they soon spread to, and flourished, in the Southern states as well, where singing instruction had not been readily available outside the upper class. Singing schools remained popular well into the mid-1800s, but began to decline in popularity, especially in the North, with the inclusion of free music instruction in the public schools (referred to as common schools) of New England. While the collapse of the singing school occurred in large part because of the advent of public school music, it is likely the singing school phenomena was largely responsible for the early success of public school music as both the first school music teachers and methods came from the singing school model.

Common Schools

The common school movement, which began during the 1820s, was one of the first ventures into public schools in the United States. The term "common school" meant to indicate schooling was available for all, and not just for certain social classes or religions. Instead of tuition being charged to attend a common school, funding came from taxation of the community served by the school. Most early common schools included instruction for students aged six to 14 or 15, and were held in a single room where one teacher provided instruction to all students at the same time. While there was a good deal of variety in the size and quality of these early public schools, the subjects studied tended to be mostly vocational in nature, centering on skills required for young adults at the time.

As the public school movement began to grow, music was still not taught as a regular subject even though it was included in many private schools at the time. The first instance of public school music was in Boston during the 1837–1838 school year. In 1836, The Boston School Committee appointed a special committee on music. The ultimate recommendation of this special committee was for the inclusion of vocal music on an experimental basis. This recommendation was based on three utilitarian rationales. First, that the study of music included *intellectual* understandings; second, that music has a connection to the *moral* feelings of man; and third, that singing, as a *physical* exercise, was valuable for medical and health reasons.

Lowell Mason, a leading proponent of music education as well as a musician and singing school teacher, volunteered his services to teach vocal music at the Hawes School in South Boston that school year. At the conclusion of the year, and in part based on Mason's success, the Boston School Committee voted to appoint a teacher of vocal music in the public schools of Boston. This was probably the first time music became an official part of the curriculum in the public schools of the United States. Mason was appointed superintendent of music in Boston, and by 1844 he and some ten other teachers were teaching vocal music in 16 Boston schools. By the start of the Civil War vocal music instruction had spread to common schools in several states across the United States.

Secondary Schools

Through the 1860s most common schools included instruction only through the seventh or eighth grade. Since vocal music instruction had become accepted by this time in many common schools, it was generally included in secondary schools as they were slowly added. The end of the Civil War brought a wide interest in instrumental music as professional concert bands and orchestras toured the country and many town bands were formed. Instrumental music first found its way into the public schools of the United States as extracurricular ensembles in the secondary schools. Students in these ensembles usually learned to play their instruments at home or from a private teacher and joined a school ensemble when it met outside the regular school day. By the turn of the century, however, bands and orchestras were becoming regular curricular subjects. By 1920 music had a firm footing in the public schools of the United States: choral music resulting from the popular singing school movement, and instrumental music influenced by the bands and orchestras that were touring the country.

Another school music ensemble that became increasingly popular after 1900 was the marching band. Marching bands originated with the military but soon became an important aspect of secondary school music programs. One of the most prominent early leaders of the school marching band movement was Austin A. Harding (1880–1958), who became the director of the University of Illinois band in 1905. His work at Illinois became a model for both college and high school marching bands across the country. During the first half of the twentieth century, the marching band became a significant public relations tool for schools. The marching band's role in the schools today continues to involve public relations, but starting in the 1970s marching band contests added a competitive element for some schools.

Pause for Reflection

Popular music of the time had a significant influence when music instruction first entered schools in the United States. Singing schools turned into choral singing in public schools. Touring bands and orchestras impacted the start of public school instrumental music. Compare this to the current relationship between popular culture and school music. What has led to the present situation? Why might this be of some concern for our profession? What might we do about this?

At the start of the twentieth century a mixture of musical cultures from Africa and Europe helped create a style that came to be called jazz. Jazz is considered by many to be the original "American" music as it was birthed in and around New Orleans, which was a major sea port at the time and was a natural place for the mixture of cultures to occur. Jazz music was slow to enter the school curriculum, but it would begin to make an appearance in schools by the late 1930s. It really wasn't until the 1960s, however, that widespread acceptance of jazz was found in the public schools. Jazz initially entered the schools in the form of instrumental groups (bands), often called stage bands, but vocal jazz has since found a strong footing in certain areas of the country.

Music Conferences and Projects

By the 1930s music was a fixture in the public schools of the United States. Music education had become a profession, with a relatively standard offering of choral, band, and orchestra classes in schools (soon to include jazz), a national professional organization, and teacher training programs offered in select institutions of higher education.

However, after World War II a school reform movement swept the United States, beginning a trend that would continue in one form or another until the present.

In 1957 the Soviet Union launched Sputnik 1, the first Earth-orbiting satellite. Resulting panic in the United States led to increased interest in science education, and the federal government began large granting programs for science, engineering, and mathematics education programs (current day "STEM" without technology yet). Private organizations, such as the National Science Foundation, also began awarding large sums of money for educational research and applications. This increased attention to specific subjects helped establish those subjects as being "basic" for all students. The arts, of course, weren't much of a player in this movement, and we have since been involved with advocacy efforts hoping to convince decision makers of our importance in education. Several conferences and projects in music education resulted, with goals to both increase the quality of music in schools and to better clarify the role of music in the schools. What follows is a quick overview of these.

Young Composers Project

Between 1959 and 1968, MENC was involved placing almost 80 young composers in schools and scheduling 16 workshops at various colleges around the county to help in-service teachers better understand contemporary music so they might make more use of new compositions in their classrooms.

Contemporary Music Project

CMP stimulated interest in comprehensive musicianship where the relationships of various aspects of music are studied in combinations instead of separately. A four-day seminar on comprehensive musicianship was sponsored by the Contemporary Music Project in 1965. The seminar was held at Northwestern University and was attended by music scholars, educators, theorists, composers, historians, and performers. Basic principles for comprehensive musicianship were established and tested at six regional Institutes for Music in Contemporary Education.

Yale Seminar on Music Education

In 1963, 31 participants, including musicians, scholars, and teachers, gathered to consider the problems facing music education and to propose possible solutions. The main question the seminar attendees addressed regarded the failure of public school music programs to produce a musically literate and active society. Several recommendations resulted from the Yale Seminar, many having to do with broadening and expanding aspects of the profession.

The Manhattanville Music Curriculum Program

The Manhattanville Music Curriculum Program (MMCP) began in 1965 to advance principles of comprehensive musicianship. The objectives of the program included the development of a sequential music curriculum for grades 3 to 12. This curriculum was based on a creative approach where children encounter stages of exploration and creativity (spiral curriculum), and they have multiple opportunities for composing, performing, conducting, listening, and evaluating.

Tanglewood Symposium

A two-week long symposium was held in 1967 at the Tanglewood Music Center in Tanglewood, Massachusetts in an effort to improve music education and to make school music study more useful to the general society. A resulting "Declaration" reported the conclusions of the two weeks of meetings. Among other things the music educators at Tanglewood[1] agreed that

> music of all periods, styles, forms, and cultures belongs in the curriculum. The musical repertory should be expanded to involve music of our time in its rich variety, including currently popular teenage music and avant-garde music, American folk music, and the music of other cultures,

and that "greater emphasis should be placed on helping the individual student to fulfill his needs, goals, and potentials."

The Goals and Objectives Project

The Goals and Objectives Project (GO Project) was begun in 1969 in efforts to implement the recommendations of the Tanglewood Symposium. This project led to the development of the 1974 publication of "The School Music Program: Description and Standards" which was a precursor of the "National Standards for Arts Education," published in 1994, and revised as the 2014 Opportunity to Learn Standards.

Federal Government and Education

More recently, the U.S. Government has taken on a greater role in the public schools. It is important to understand that education, in the United States, is under state and local control. The federal government, for the most part, has little to do with how schools function and what is taught in them. However, the federal government can wield considerable influence by providing funding for states and local school districts that implement specific requirements. States can opt out of federal requirements, but it comes at the loss of potential significant funding. There have been several recent examples of this, with the "Goals 2000: Educate America Act" having the most important impact on music education.

The Goals 2000 Act (P. L. 103–227) was signed into law on March 31, 1994, by President Bill Clinton. It provided funding to states and local communities to help assure that students reach higher levels of achievement. This was an important law for arts and music education in that it listed the arts as a core subject along with English, math, history, civics and government, geography, science, and foreign language. A direct result of the Goals 2000 Act was the creation of the National Standards for Arts Education which included nine music content standards that defined what students should know and be able to do.

The National Standards for music had a significant impact on music teaching and learning, especially at the elementary school level where many music teachers adopted a mixture of the nine contact standards into their teaching. Among other things, this resulted in the introduction of creative experiences for students as teachers added more composition and improvisation activities. Many secondary school music teachers, however, resisted implementing standards outside of those dealing with performance and music reading.

In 2014, NAfME revised the National Music Standards. The new standards are meant to cultivate a student's understanding of the artistic processes of creating, performing, and responding. A separate listing of standards was created for PK-8 general music, composition/theory, music technology, guitar/keyboard/harmonizing instruments, and ensemble. (You can access these standards at www.nafme.org/my-classroom/standards/core-music-standards/.)

The Present

By the start of the twenty-first century there existed a relatively standardized music education model within the various public school systems across the United States. Secondary School music programs have retained the same band, choral, and orchestral performance ensembles that were established around the start of the twentieth century. At most secondary schools one can find various concert, marching, and jazz bands (as well as regionally relevant groups such as mariachi bands, steel drum bands, African drumming ensembles, and polka bands), mixed choirs, single gender choirs (men's chorus and women's chorus), and/or jazz choirs, full and/or string orchestras.

With very few exceptions, all these ensembles function in similar ways. Each ensemble typically convenes several times a week and prepares music for concerts. Most tend to be curricular, meaning they meet during the regular school day and students receive academic credit for participating. It is not uncommon, however, to find some ensembles that meet before and/or after school hours, and students "volunteer" to participate. Quite often marching bands exist as a kind of co-curricular class that meets both during the school day as well as before or after school. While certainly not every secondary school has classes of bands, choirs, and orchestras, the greater majority do have at least one of these types of performing ensembles.

Even though these traditional ensemble classes dominate music instruction in American secondary schools, other music classes can be found in some schools. Music theory classes are not uncommon, primarily in high schools, and will often prepare students for a music theory Advanced Placement test – popular especially for students with an interest in being a music major in college. Various types of music history or music appreciation courses are offered in some schools, with topics ranging from traditional Western European history to the history of rock and roll. Private or small group lessons are taught in elementary and secondary schools in some parts of the country. Other classes that seem to be catching on in schools include guitar classes, music technology and/or recording classes, and electronic piano classes. Some schools have added new performance opportunities that specialize in rock, rap, and/or hip-hop musics including programs such as Little Kids Rock and Modern Band.[2] However, even with this variety of courses, the mainstay of music education in American secondary schools remains the traditional bands, choruses, and orchestras.

Elementary school music experiences across much of the country, while certainly not identical, most often have several characteristics in common. Students in the elementary grades are usually required to take a music course during most, if not all, school years. It is important to note, however, that there are school districts across the country that have eliminated elementary music instruction altogether. Unlike in secondary schools, an elementary student does not normally attend music class every day. If fact, it is quite rare for a student to attend a music class more than once or twice per week. Some schools are even on six-, seven-, or eight-day rotations so that a particular student wouldn't even receive weekly music instruction. Music classes can meet for about an hour or as little as 25 minutes at a time. Additionally, there is a great variety in teaching conditions across the elementary schools in the United States. Some schools provide their music teacher(s) with a specialized facility for music teaching, often equipped with a wide array of musical instruments and technologies, while other schools do not have a "music room" but require their music teacher to travel to individual classrooms carrying, or carting with them, whatever equipment they have.

The curriculum of most elementary music programs tends to be quite similar in that there are attempts made to address many of the nine content areas of the original National Standards from 1994, and more recently the new 2014 Standards. The actual methods of teaching can differ widely, however, usually based on the training an individual teacher has received. It is quite common for elementary music instruction to include significant performance experience through singing and playing of instruments that might include small percussion instruments, barred instruments, recorders, various drums, and body percussion instruments and sounds. Movement activities are also typical, as are music listening experiences. Most elementary music teachers consider it very important to develop music reading and writing skills, so activities to foster these are commonplace as well. While probably still not as extensive as most of these other experiences, the inclusion of compositional and improvisational activities has grown more prevalent since the mid-1990s. Other involvements that are now frequent include opportunities to experience a diverse range of musics, including use of classic and popular world musics, popular music from the United States, and various digital technologies.

Another important aspect of elementary school music experience is ensemble participation. Often in addition to the music class, students will be afforded opportunities to rehearse and perform in ensembles. Many schools will offer a mixture of different types of choirs and instrumental groups for which students can select and/or audition. The variety of instrumental opportunities has grown recently to include hand bell choirs, recorder ensembles, steel drum ensembles, guitar ensembles, rock bands, African drumming ensembles, etc. More often than not, these ensembles follow the same model as do secondary school ensembles, where most (if not all) of their time together is spent rehearsing for concerts.

As we move through the third decade of the twenty-first century, the teaching of music has certainly been well established in the schools of the United States. We are, however, witnessing a reduction in music teaching positions in various school systems across the country as both music enrollments and education budgets shrink. Large ensemble performance remains the dominate musical involvement, with teaching in elementary schools including more breadth than depth, and secondary schools primarily dealing with depth instead of breadth. Finally, it is important to notice that many of the recommendations resulting from the conferences and programs in the 1960s have still not been addressed in any significant way by the profession. More than 50 years after the Yale Seminar, the Tanglewood Symposium, and the GO Project, we continue struggling to develop music programs for all students that correlate performing, creating, and listening. We still grapple with the inclusion of musics from popular styles and new technologies, and we have yet to find serious ways to help individual students fulfill specific needs, goals, and potentials. As a profession, we have come a long way, but there is still much to do.

Pause for Reflection

What differences do you think might there be between high school music programs across the country? What about middle school programs? What about elementary school music programs? Do you think there should be more similarity or more diversity within individual schools? Why?

Notes

1   Robert Choate, ed., "Documentary Report of the Tanglewood Symposium" (Washington, DC: Music Educators National Conference, 1968), p. 139.
2   Little Kids Rock (and Modern Band) is a national nonprofit that provides training and resources to public school teachers interested in bringing experiences with popular music to school programs. (See www.littlekidsrock. org/.)

Readings and References

Birge, E. B. (1966). *History of Public School Music in the United States*, new and augmented edition. Reston, VA: MENC: The National Association for Music Education.

Bruner, J. (1977). *The Process of Education*. Cambridge, MA: Harvard University Press.

Choksy, L. Abramson, R. M., Gillespie, A. E., Woods, D., and York, F. (2001). *Teaching Music in the Twenty-First Century*. Upper Saddle River, NJ: Prentice Hall.

Dewey, J. (1998). *Experience and Education*, 60th anniversary edition. Indianapolis: IN: Kappa Delta Pi.

Mark, M. L. and Gary, C. L. (2007). *A History of American Music Education*, 3rd ed. Reston, VA: MENC: The National Association for Music Education.

3　Societal Change

I hope Chapter 2 gave you a perspective on how our profession got its start, and a better idea of what our profession looks like today. It's very important to understand what has happened in our past, and what is going on presently, as it makes us better qualified to make judgments about our future. I suggested in Chapter 1 that this book is, more than anything else, about change. A number of phenomenon have occurred, and are occurring, to create a time that is ripe (and right) for change in the music education profession. I would argue that change isn't just a good thing we could do, but something that is absolutely necessary.

Let's get right to the "why?" question. After all, there are some really extraordinary things about music education in the United States. Most importantly is the very model on which our profession is based – the traditional performing ensemble. In many respects, this model has been quite successful. The performance level of our ensembles has been envied by music teachers in several countries. It has served important roles of public relations and service for schools. It has sustained the profession and has become a prominent part of the secondary school experience and for many elementary schools as well. The traditional ensemble model has, in fact, become synonymous with music education in schools. So much so, that it is difficult for most music educators, as well as pre-service music teachers like yourself, to consider changes to the status quo. But the call for change is now well established. David Hebert (2009), who has published in the areas of musicology, sociomusicology, and music education suggests,

> Wind bands, choirs, and orchestras have long served as a staple of school music education in the United States, but this large ensemble model has for good reason met criticism in recent years as progressive music educators contemplate ways that music education might be re-envisioned in order to become more effective and meaningful in students' musical lives in, outside of, and after graduation from school. Questions have been raised regarding the extent

to which large performance ensembles might or should continue to hold a prominent position in the future of school music education. Specifically, what are their unique advantages, and what of importance is missing from the typical large ensemble experience that might be imparted through the use of new approaches or even entirely different forms of music teaching?

(Hebert 2009, p. 40)

You might be thinking to yourself "if it ain't broke, don't fix it." I'm going to suggest that while our traditional ensemble model might not be "broke," it is certainly falling short in different ways. There are several issues we need to consider carefully as we begin to think about the future of music education.

Musical Culture in the U.S.

Let's first consider what American musical culture was like when ensembles began achieving success in schools. As discussed in Chapter 2, choral ensembles in public schools were the direct outgrowth of the singing schools. Singing was a valued aspect of society and was regarded as useful for all citizens. With this backdrop it was only natural that music in the schools began with singing and vocal ensembles.

Beginning around the end of the Civil War, instrumental music, which included professional concert bands and orchestras, was also quite popular. This popularity, to some degree, stemmed from the fact that many people did not have daily opportunities to hear music. The only method to hear music on a regular basis was performing it yourself, or with family and friends. Radio and the phonograph were both in their infancy, so the touring professional music ensemble was a much needed form of entertainment. Given the musical society at the time, can you imagine how appealing an opportunity to play in such a musical ensemble might have been?

The popularity of bands and orchestras in American culture helped to establish the same type of ensembles as features of public schools. The rise of instrumental music in the public schools, especially with wind and string instruments, was a natural outgrowth of American musical culture at the time.

Pause for Reflection

The number one popular song of 1920 was "Dardanella" recorded by Ben Selvin's Orchestra. The number one song of 1930 was "Stein Song" recorded by Rudy Vallee. Listen to these songs (YouTube will have them). Listen to other songs by these groups, and other groups at the time. What is your first reaction to this sound? What do you hear? What about popular music has changed since this time?

A lot has happened since then ... The automobile became the desired mode of transportation, and people were able to travel distances with relative ease, allowing them to attend a wider variety of activities. The radio became a common component of households, permitting both live and recorded music into the home. You could actually sit in your living room and enjoy the NBC Symphony Orchestra under the direction of Arturo Toscanini. You could also hear Patti Page sing the *Tennessee Waltz*, and Red Foley's *Chattanooga Shoe Shine Boy*. The television later replaced the radio in the living room permitting people to see musicians as well as hear them. You could now sit in your house and watch Leonard Bernstein conduct the New York Philharmonic.

You could also catch Elvis on the Ed Sullivan show. Speaking of Elvis, there was a new style of music that appeared toward the middle of the 1950s. This music popularized the guitar, which became the electric guitar. It also featured a drummer playing a set of drums, a bass guitar, and quite often an electronic organ. The music was called rock and roll (you may have heard of it). While there were a good number of rock songs that employed traditional wind and string instruments, rock music was about plugging in and playing loud and so the focus was seldom on the more traditional instruments. During the 1980s, and on, the use of wind and string instruments in rock music styles moved more and more to the fringes of this music.

Rock music isn't just about the music – it's a show. Rock concerts are as much a visual event as they are a auditory affair. By contrast, the focus of the musical styles used in schools is squarely on the music itself. Performers primarily sit or stand still, and the audience is to sit quietly and listen. However, rock concerts include movement, audience interaction, clapping, cheering, lights, smoke, fireworks, and on, and on. The "show" is as much a part of the musical experience as is the music. This showmanship feature of rock and roll was fundamental in the popularization of the music video. Music videos of rock music performances have been used for several purposes, but they have proven to be an important aspect of this music.

Other cultural changes have occurred since bands, choirs, and orchestras were included in the schools. The professional concert bands disappeared. The professional orchestras all but stopped touring, and more recently they are disappearing as well. By the 1980s popular interest in jazz music had evaporated and most of the big bands that popularized swing music had dissolved. Jazz currently remains at the fringes of popular culture.

Other musical changes have happened. Electronic synthesizers began appearing on recordings in the late 1960s, and the new sounds of which these instruments were capable became prominent in popular music. Of course, this was only the beginning. Soon, synthesizers were joined by samplers and a whole host of digital instruments. Digital and electronic sounds became very popular across different styles of music. Samplers have been used to replace more traditional instruments as well. The use of traditional wind and string instruments in studio recordings and in live performance steadily decreased as sampling technologies improved.

There is one more societal change we need to address. That is the internet. The internet is all about change, and it will continue to change most everything we do. It has changed the way we interact, the way we learn, the way we shop, the way we live. The internet has even helped change time, as we expect things to happen faster as our attention span grows shorter. It is also changing our interactions with music. It has already changed the way we buy and sell music. It has changed the way you can learn about music. It is changing how music can be taught. It is changing the definition of music performance. It is changing the way people interact musically. Much too often I hear music teachers talk about the internet as something that isn't of much use to them as far as teaching goes. The standard line is "you can't do 'that' over the internet," and we continue as if the internet is a fad that won't affect us. I'm afraid what we perceive as limitations of the internet are more about our own limitations. It would be comforting to go on with our business ignoring the potential of the internet, but that would not be wise. None of us can imagine what the internet will become and what will be possible with it in the future, but you can be sure that it will continue to change how we do things. It will continue to change the way we do music, and it would be a big mistake to ignore what is being done with music over the internet. We will return to this topic later in the book and look at a few possibilities.

Music Technology Changes

At this point we must back up and look at the impact the phonograph had on musical culture. As previously discussed, before the invention of sound recording technologies, live music was the only music. I have to say that again. Not just for effect, but because it is so foreign to us today. *Live music was the only music!* You have to think about that for a minute … The main way to experience music was as a performer yourself, so just about everyone was, to some extent, a musical performer.

The phonograph changed that. With the availability of recorded music it was no longer necessary to make music personally. Instead, you could just listen to a recording. This made musics available that most people would have never encountered live, and it changed the way our society experienced music. Today, after more than 100 years of improvements in sound recording, we are a society of music listeners, with a very low percentage of people who regularly perform music in any substantive way. It was an advance in technology that changed the musical interactions of an entire society. This history is important to understand, as it is happening again.

Today we are living during the early stages of another technology that is changing the way our society interacts with music. Digital technologies have brought musical possibilities to the general public that not many years ago were available only to a select group of professionals, and at a cost that is a fraction of what it once was. Almost anyone, young and old, can now perform music, and be fairly good at it after a short period of time. Almost anyone, young and old, can now compose music, and be fairly good at it after a short period of time. Almost anyone, young and old, can now improvise music, and be fairly good at it after a short period of time.

Also, the capabilities to combine composition, improvisation, performance, and listening (not to mention sampling, recording, mixing, and producing) into one action is now possible. These musical processes have historically been separated, but today, with the help of digital technologies, they can easily be done together. Keep in mind, this is a very young technology (just because something has been available *your* entire life, doesn't mean it has always been this way). The distinction between "musician" and "non-musician" is certainly blurring more and more, and we have no way of knowing where this will take us in 50 years (or even five)!

It's important to address a couple concerns you are probably having with these new found possibilities (these won't be your last concerns we deal with!). Let's first explore the ease by which people can now make music. It doesn't seem right, does it? After all, you spent years slaving away in practice rooms to achieve a quality performance level. But now, new technologies take a lot of that away. Seemingly, with a simple touch, music pours out. Gone is most of the agonizing over technique, the concern about intonation, the necessity of notational skills. This makes performance seem cheapened somehow. Let's look at this from a different perspective – one that might not hit so close to home for you.

I'm sure when the metal pen first appeared there was great anguish from a lot of people who didn't want to believe this new technology should replace the quill as a writing instrument. It must have seemed too easy. Gone was the agonizing over selecting feathers, the concern about curing and cutting quills, the necessity of cleaning and hardening. I'm sure this made writing seem cheapened somehow. So, what's your take on this technology? Are you interested in going back to gathering feathers, curing and cutting them, cleaning, hardening, dipping … it might have some romanticized appeal, but you would probably tire of it quickly. Certainly there are people who still write with quills today, but for the general public, technology has made writing a more meaningful experience (and of course, it didn't stop with the metal pen). I would imagine many individuals involved with the quill trade had a choice to make. They could change and adapt to new ways of doing things, or they may have been forced out of a job.

There is a similarity with music composition. Today, anyone can be a composer. With the aid of the right technologies, elementary school children (and younger) can create new music. Do they need to know how to "write" music first? No! Don't they need to understand instrument ranges? Not necessary! What about an understanding of parallel fifths? Forget about it! That can't be right, can it?

I have to tell you a personal story. It's one of my favorites these days, and it happens to be true! When I first went to college I was a clarinet player. That's what I knew; that's what defined me. But when it came time to pick classes my first semester I noticed that music composition was offered, so I asked if I could take it. The answer was, "Not until you take music theory first." Ok, I took a year of music theory, and then I asked if I could take music composition. The answer was, "Not until you take music theory III and IV." Ok, I took another year of music theory. Then I thought I had them … I looked at all the available music classes and there was no theory V, so I asked if I could take music composition. The answer was, "Not until you take Form and Analysis and Orchestration." Turns out they were smarter than I was and picked better names for these "advanced" theory courses. Well, that's the end of the story. By that time I didn't care about composing any longer. They had won. After all, composing is something really special of which very few people are capable … right? Not at all. Creativity in music could very well be what it's all about! You shouldn't need three years of music theory classes before you can begin making creative decisions with sound. And you shouldn't have to play an instrument for three years before you can begin making creative decisions with sound. We should be involving students with creative problem solving from the very beginning. Making use of new technologies can help students get to creative moments quickly as it frees students from many of the burdens that we have traditionally imposed on them.

Consider the following from Peter Webster (1990), a leading researcher in creative thinking and music education technology. While some of the terminology is now dated, it demonstrates the range of amazing possibilities.

> Imagine a child seated at a music keyboard with a computer screen providing the score. This child composes a brief fragment of music by playing on the music keyboard. This fragment is displayed on the screen (in traditional notation or in other forms) and is played through speakers. The child continues to expand the fragment, working with many different timbres, additional voices, dynamics, and phrase patterns. At one point the child becomes frustrated and quits, saving the work in a file. The child returns later to the saved composition and continues work until a final version is ready to be shared with the teacher and the class. The child then prints a copy of the score and takes it home for the refrigerator door, and transfers the recording to cassette tape for the child's parents to hear. Throughout the entire process, the computer has saved every moment of the child's work and can "replay" the "electronic sketches" in exacting detail ... Just a few years ago, such a scenario would have seemed financially and technologically out of the question. Not so today. With software and hardware to support multimedia applications, music work stations of this sort now exist in music labs in several schools. Similar projects will be easily designed by the teacher for performers and listeners as well. This technology will soon help us to expand our understanding of musical imagination, to challenge our concepts of the creative process, and to measure and observe creative thinking in ways never thought possible.

Improved music technologies are creating a never-ending cascade of new opportunities for music education. Taking advantage of these opportunities will mean making changes in the way music education has been approached. If you don't like it, you can stomp your feet and proclaim the virtues of the "old way." However, change will continue, and our culture will continue to transform. Just like individuals long ago in the quill trade, you will have choices to make – adapt or risk being left behind.

This brings us to the second concern you may have with the possibilities created by new technologies, and that has to do with the role of the teacher. If technology makes music performance and composition so easy and assessable, can't people just do music on their own now? Do we still need music teachers? I suggest the answer to both these questions is "yes." Yes, most anyone can make music with the assistance of new technologies, and yes, we still need music teachers. Regardless of the technology (remember that the oboe is a technology) the intention should not be to "teach" the technology, but to use the technology to make music. Notwithstanding which technology is being used, the teacher's primary job is to help students develop musicality, and there is certainly no indication this job will be replaced anytime soon. New technologies only create new ways of going about doing what we did before – helping students create music. They don't replace what we did before, but instead make it different. Remember the primary topic of this book? It's about "change." Yes, there is a real need for music teachers, but the role of the teacher will need to change as the technology makes changes in the discipline.

We are living during a time of amazing change in the way our society does music. Just like the phonograph changed people's interactions with musical sounds beginning over 100 years ago, digital music is having a profound effect on musical experiences in our society today. So, what does this have to do with you as a future music teacher? Simply put, it is unwise to just assume music making in schools can continue as it always has without any regard to students' lives outside of school. In the early 1900s the musical values in schools closely resembled the musical values of students outside of schools. This is no longer the case.[1] The American philosopher and educational reformer, John Dewey,[1] discussing the necessity to reassess values that at one time seemed ideal, warns: "in a moving world, solidification is always dangerous." He would later add, "The business of reflection in determining the true good cannot be done once for all ... It needs to be done, and done over and over and over again, in terms of the conditions of concrete situations as they arise. In short, the need for reflection and insight is perpetually recurring."

Wayne Bowman (2009) recommends that the value of music education is closely tied to the values of music in society, and as such should have relevance for the general population. He suggests,

> the values of music and music education are always socially and politically modulated, and are relative to the ways they serve human living. Rather than straight-ahead affairs whose value is absolute and invariably positive, music and music education require utmost sensitivity to situational variables, and constant, critical reassessment.
>
> (Bowman 2009, p. 5)

School Change

Another change is the term "school." After the 1920s, school had become a pretty standardized thing. Schools were buildings with students learning and teachers teaching, all in a pretty consistent manner. It isn't too reductionist to say there were public schools and there were private schools. Pretty simple. It's not so simple anymore. Now there are public schools, private schools, pre-schools, magnet schools, charter schools, home schools, online schools, continuing education schools, trade schools, professional schools, and on. Additionally, there are English as a second language learners, special learners, gifted learners, urban education, standardized testing, and pay for performance issues. I'm sure I left something out, but you probably get the picture.

Then there are changes to what has been considered good educational practice. Educational and psychological theories that have evolved since the 1950s have had significant impact on what education in schools looks like, or should look like. Work in cognitive science, experiential learning, inquiry-based science, and constructivist theories[2] has questioned traditional approaches to education. A constructionist teacher, for example, often takes on a role of facilitator (learner-centered pedagogy) rather than that of a traditional teacher who would impart information (teacher-centered pedagogy). This allows students to make use of the previous knowledge and experience they bring with them into the classroom as they draw conclusions from their own creative problem solving. By standing back and allowing students to experiment, teachers enable more natural modes of learning to take place, typically in a hands-on, student-centered way. This does not look much like what music teachers have traditionally done, but perhaps it is something you should know more about. We'll return to this topic a little later as well.

So let's recap somewhat. At the start of this chapter I suggested change in the practice of music education wouldn't be just a good thing, but something that is absolutely necessary. Then we reviewed some of what has changed in our society since traditional ensemble performance became the fundamental way of doing music in the schools: technology changed the primary musical involvement from performance to listening; the automobile replaced the horse for transportation; the radio brought music into homes; the television brought music with images into the home; rock and roll flourished; concerts became shows; video became popular; professional concert bands disappeared; professional orchestras suffered; jazz feel out of popular favor; electronic music arrived; digital music followed; the internet opened up the world; attention spans became shorter; and new educational psychologies challenged traditional pedagogical methods. It's been over 100 years. Society has changed. Music has changed. Schools have changed. The way our society does music has changed. But the foundation of music in the schools has not changed. While the model of education in music made sense as we moved into the twentieth century, it is vital we examine the possibilities as we continue through the twenty-first.

Pause for Reflection

On the surface all this talk about change seems pretty distressing and negative. What might be the positives that could result from change?

Music Education Elephants

There is a growing concern within our profession about the future of K-12 music education programs and much of the anxiety involves enrollment in traditional ensembles. The concern is so great we spend a considerable amount of time trying to convince others of the importance of music through advocacy efforts. In the introduction to her chapter on advocacy, in *The New Handbook of Research on Music Teaching and Learning*, Liora Bresler (2002, p. 1066) suggests: "the contemporary arena of school music often resembles a battleground, concerned with survival." I believe we may be spending so much time advocating for what we do, that we can't spend enough time considering what it is we are doing. In Chapter 1, I mentioned that our profession has a few elephants that we simply don't like to talk about. The backbone of our profession, the large performance ensemble, may be our biggest elephant, and a significant reason for our advocacy needs.

I suggest the issue isn't the ensembles themselves, but instead *our seemingly singular devotion to this model with its teacher-centric pedagogy.* Usually, when this issue is raised among music educators, defensiveness results. It is little wonder this traditional ensemble model remains so ubiquitous in the United States. It is, after all, the model that practically all current music teachers experienced as students. It is the only model in which most college music education majors participated during their secondary school years, and continue throughout their undergraduate experience. It is, in fact, the model in which most in-service and pre-service teachers not only participated, but excelled. Bringing to others the same triumphs we experienced is quite gratifying, and is an aspiration that drives many to become music teachers. It is very difficult, for those who are products of this traditional ensemble system, to imagine loyalty to the quintessential music class as being problematic.

So, this brings up several questions. Do we replace traditional ensembles with something else? Do we keep our ensembles, and add something else as well? Do we try to change the traditional ensemble model? Do we change and add? Do we stick our heads in the sand and ignore our reality? I'd vote "yes" four times, and then "no" once. We can no longer afford ignoring the cultural changes that have occurred over the past 100 plus years and how these impact our traditional music teaching model. But voting yes four times means things could get complex. This means that various schools could have different models of music education. One school might not offer traditional ensembles at all, but instead have a variety of unconventional music classes, perhaps taught using primarily a leaner-centered pedagogical approach. Another school might have a traditional ensemble program along with some alternatives. Yet another school might offer traditional ensemble classes in unorthodox ways. There is so much diversity in the United States that it would seem diversity in music education would be welcomed. What works at one school might founder at another. A lot of this would have to do with the realities at a given school. I'm suggesting that you need to be prepared to stretch yourself, especially if you decided to become a music education major simply because you want to direct traditional ensembles in secondary schools.

Daniel Cavicchi (2009) warns that students are conscious of a "peculiar kind of separation between music in school and music outside of school. The musical activities and behaviors that students take for granted as they go about their lives in the modern world are suddenly rather meaningless when they enter the music classroom and vice versa" (p. 98). I worry that if you continue *only* down the traditional music education path there is a good chance you will be disappointed when you begin teaching. Our society has changed too much, and the changes continue. I suspect a lot of young music teachers leave the profession after only a few years of teaching, in some part, because they were not prepared for the musical perspectives that students bring into schools. I want you to be prepared. I want you to anticipate the vast richness, and the variety of musical interests students bring to school with them, and I want you to have strategies for how you might best deal with all the musical realities that await you.

Pause for Reflection

Let's assume upon graduation you take a job as a middle school band director. The school principal wants significantly more students enrolled in music classes. What might you do to make this a reality? For what kinds of help might you ask the principal?

Traditional Ensembles

Before we move on to how the profession might change, let's talk about what we don't want to lose from our traditional approach to music education. I suggest there are two very important features of ensemble performance that we should attempt to maintain, no matter what. First is a very high quality of group performance. Probably above all else, music teachers have developed ensembles that display astounding levels of musicianship. Improving students' musicianship skills should be a goal of any musical experience offered in schools. However, it is important to understand that musicianship can be manifested in several ways. Historically, while ignoring musicality as it exists in society at large, we have engaged with music almost exclusively through a particular type of performance, with particular styles of music. Cavicchi (2009) suggests

> the bifurcation of music in daily life and music education is rooted more deeply in conflicting ideas about musicality. Music institutions promote a means of "being musical" which is quite narrowly defined when compared to the musical actions and experiences of most people as they wake, commute, work, shop, relax, and otherwise pass the time in a complex, modern society.
>
> (Cavicchi 2009, p. 99)

While musicianship must remain a high priority, the breadth of musicianship skills we make available must be broadened as we consider various types of musical experiences for the schools.

Second, we must maintain the group dynamics and social aspects of ensemble participation. Students consistently report that their enjoyment in school music ensembles is tied in substantial ways to the social interactions between members of the group. Learning is also fostered by and through this sense of community. It must be pointed out, however, that the impact of social interactions is no less important in most, if not all, school group activities. We can't say, for example, that relationships developed through participation in girls' volleyball teams, student government, or chess clubs, are less meaningful than music ensemble participation. Regardless, the importance of social interactions should not be understated and must be preserved in most all school musical experiences.

Change. Today it seems to be an inevitable aspect of life. Of course, this is nothing new as the twentieth century witnessed staggering changes. What's more, the rate of change continues to increase as we move through the twenty-first century. Just about every facet of life in our society has evidenced change, including the ways in which music is experienced. Yet with all this as background, the music education profession keeps churning away as if it was 1920 again. We continue in this way at our own peril, and that simply can't be an option. In Chapter 4, I will present some opportunities for change in which our profession might take advantage. Opportunities that, if taken, would make what we do more relevant to the students we serve, as well as to our society in general. While any of these opportunities could be applied to our traditional performance offerings, I believe they are a better fit for other types of music classes – in some cases classes that might not already exist in many schools. Then in Chapter 5, I will suggest some specifics about these types of music classes.

Notes

1 From *The Essential Dewey, Volume 1, Pragmatism, Education, and Democracy* (1998), edited by Larry A. Hickman and Thomas M. Alexander, p. 90; and, *The Later Works of John Dewey, Volume 7: 1932, Ethics* (2008), edited by Jo Ann Boydston, p. 212.
2 There are a wealth of writings concerning work in cognitive science, experiential learning, inquiry-based science and constructivist theories. For an excellent introduction to these ideas, see Piaget's *Science of Education and Psychology of the Child*. Other good source materials include Bransford, Brown and Cocking's *How People Learn*, Lambert and McCombs *How Students Learn*, and Mayer's *Learning and Instruction*.

Readings and References

Bowman, W. D. (2009). No one true way: Music education without redemptive truth. In Regelski, T. A. and Gates, J. T. (eds.), *Music Education for Changing Times: Guiding Visions for Practice*; Landscapes: the Arts, Aesthetics, and Education series, Volume 7. New York: Springer.

Bransford, J. D., Brown, A. L., and Cocking, R. R. (eds.). (1999). *How People Learn*. Washington, DC: National Academy Press.

Bresler, L. (2002). Research: A foundation for the arts education advocacy. In R. Colwell and C. Richardson (eds.), *The New Handbook of Research on Music Teaching and Learning*. New York: Oxford University Press, pp. 1066–1083.

Bruer, J. T. (1993). *Schools for Thought: A Science of Learning in the Classroom*. Cambridge, MA: MIT Press.

Cavicchi, D. (2009). My music, their music, and the irrelevance of music education. In Regelski, T. A. and Gates, J. T. (eds.), *Music Education for Changing Times: Guiding Visions for Practice*; Landscapes: the Arts, Aesthetics, and Education series, Volume 7. New York: Springer.

Elpus, K. and Abril, C. R. (2011). High school music ensemble students in the United States: A demographic profile. *Journal of Research in Music Education*, 59(2): 128–145.

Lambert, N. M. and McCombs, B. L. (eds.). (1998). *How Students Learn*. Washington, DC: American Psychological Association.

Mayer, R. E. (2003). *Learning and Instruction*. Upper Saddle River: Prentice Hall.

Piaget, J. (1970). *Science of Education and Psychology of the Child*. New York: Oxford University Press.

Steffe, L. P. and Gale, J. (eds.). (1995). *Constructivism in Education*. Mahwah, NJ: Erlbaum.

Webster, P. R. (1990). Creativity as creative thinking. *Music Educators Journal*, 76(9): 22–29.

4   Opportunities for Change

So let's get to some specifics concerning change. Considering all the societal, musical, and educational changes that have occurred during the last 100 years, it is no wonder our model of music education, which has remained remarkably unchanged during this same period of time, needs to evolve. As a profession, should our goal be to perpetuate the type of musical experience we enjoyed as students, or should we adapt as necessary to reach new generations with musical experiences that might be more meaningful and relevant to them? That may be the most important question I've asked you so far. When we are passionate about something, like many in our profession are about traditional performance ensembles, it is easy to assume everyone else is similarly infatuated. This is unfortunately not true. We know that after elementary school the greater majority of students choose not to participate in our traditional offerings, and most of them do not because they find this musical participation uninteresting. Research by McPherson and Hendricks (2010) indicated that while school-aged students in the United States showed great interest in music outside of schools, their interest level for school music ranked lower than their interest in art, PE, English, math, and science. I hope you find that shocking!

Pause for Reflection

McPherson and Hendricks' study didn't measure the numbers of students that actually participated in music, but instead, it concerned student "interest." Why do you think students are very interested in music outside of school, but not so much in school? Is this troubling? Does it matter? Why or why not?

Even many of those that do participate are less than enthusiastic about the experience. I think this is difficult for many music education majors to appreciate. After all, most music education students lived and breathed their high school musical involvement. It was important to them. They practiced. They hung around with friends that were probably excited about ensemble participation as well. If this sounds like you, you are not alone. This describes many music education majors, and this is a large part of why many students decide to major in music education in the first place. While in high school, however, these students seldom noticed how many students participating in ensembles weren't so enraptured. Most ensembles contain students that live on the margin. Sometimes, the greater majority of students fit here. They don't practice much (if at all), and they don't seem very stimulated by day to day ensemble events (like rehearsals). Some are so unmotivated you might wonder why they enroll in an ensemble in the first place. Maybe a parent swayed their decision. Maybe they had an older sibling that influenced them. Maybe they followed a boy/girl friend. Maybe they were attracted by the ensemble's reputation. Maybe they thought it would be more fun than it turned out to be. Maybe it was to avoid taking a physical education class. My oldest daughter decided to take middle school band for three years once she learned she could avoid enrolling in PE all three years. She pretty much hated the experience, but apparently it was better than PE. By the way, she wasn't alone!

Whatever the reasons, there is a notable amount of students that, although enrolled in traditional ensembles, are not really inspired by the venture. It may well be that many students participate in bands, choirs and orchestras simply because there are no other musical options available to them. We can do better than this. We must do better. It is essential that we offer interesting, relevant, and meaningful musical experiences for diverse groups of students. Experiences that also allow them to develop lifelong musical skills. For some students this will mean traditional ensembles, but for many others it will necessitate different types of music offerings. This is our challenge. As the future of music education, this is *your* challenge.

Marie McCarthy (2009) describes our challenge this way:

> As already noted, perhaps the strongest legacy of school music in the United States is its performance tradition. This tradition is surrounded by a set of values and practices, among them: technically high standards, emphasis on product, dominance of competition, hierarchies and structures similar to professional ensembles, and rankings and ratings that classify and evaluate individuals and groups ... This system of ensembles, which is deeply rooted in the professional music world, is one model for developing musicianship and musicality in children and youth. The challenge for the future is to develop new models that achieve the same goal, models grounded in the social and cultural contexts of the musical

practices they represent – from steel drum to Ghanaian drumming groups, Irish traditional music to gamelan ensembles, or mariachi to popular music bands. The structures for setting up such groups are already in place – for example, in community schools or cultural centers. A successful juxtaposition of traditional, classically based ensembles and alternative school music groups would highlight the social and cultural aspects of musical meaning and revitalize the role of music in school and community culture

(McCarthy 2009, p. 33)

Pause for Reflection

Think back to your high school experience. If there were rock music (or rap or hip-hop, etc.) classes offered, do you think they would "steal" students from the traditional ensemble classes? Why or why not? Does it matter if they would or would not?

I believe there are several opportunities for change that are worthy of serious consideration as we look to the future of music education in the United States. Many of these are interrelated with each other, as we will see, so that one opportunity is dependent on others. But I suggest change is a worthy goal. We have to be brave enough to venture into some unknown territory. We must be open to possibilities. Toward this end, in this chapter I will introduce several opportunities that are available to improve the situation in which we find ourselves. Opportunities, that when taken in combination, could help us realize interesting, relevant, educational, and meaningful musical experiences for more students than we currently serve. There is really little here (if anything) that is revolutionary. The methodologies I'm suggesting are familiar in many musical styles outside the schools, and as David Hebert (2009) attests, have been a part of school music curriculum in other countries for some time:

it is important to note that in the United Kingdom, Scandinavia and Australasia, school music education programs have for decades emphasized, particularly innovative approaches to creative musicianship, including song writing and composition, the widespread use of new technologies, and performance of popular music on characteristic instruments in schools.

(Hebert 2009, p. 43)

I want to make it clear that I am proposing these opportunities primarily for alternative types of music classes (see Chapter 5 for specific examples). While such opportunities could also be successfully applied to our traditional ensemble classes, they might change, in fundamental ways, this model of performance class. That would be quite a leap of faith for our profession, and one that I doubt will soon occur in any substantial way. Instead, I would suggest these opportunities will have the most significant influence on music education programs (including students, teachers and schools) when implemented in different types of music classes.

1) *Class Size.* "The more, the merrier." This is often the traditional view for music class size. I fear there is a misconception about the relationship between quantity and educational effectiveness. There is no guarantee learning will improve as quantity increases. Yet, having 80 enrolled in a concert chorus is usually perceived as better than having 40. Where did we get the idea that bigger is better? Instead of educational rationales, I fear it generally has more to do with concerns about survival and/or personal pride. As music enrollments drop in a school, there is greater potential a music teaching position will be cut. Generally speaking, many principals have some autonomy over which teaching positions they hire. A school's total enrollment helps dictate how many teaching positions might be available for the principal to hire, and then on average, a teacher position would equal a certain minimum number of students. As an example, for a specific school let's pretend that an average teacher position equates to 100 students (an average of five classes with 20 students each). If this pretend school presently employs two music teachers and the school enrolls 50 students in choir and another 50 in band ... well, do you see what the principal might do? A good fiscal manager (this is an important job for principals) would drop one music position, assign both band and choir to one teacher, and hire a new teacher to help with an academic area with more need. Another possibility would be to assign other classes (math, social studies, intensive reading, etc.) to the two music teachers until their teaching loads were full. So the band director might teach one class of band, two reading courses, and two classes of civics. I recently met with a local band director (her school was not pretend) who taught band and drivers' education. I bet that's not what you have in mind for your first teaching position! She was thinking, by the way, about getting out of teaching.

So there is this numbers game we have to play. You have to produce the correct numbers to stay in the game, therefore the notion of having large classes helps to meet the requirement. This all makes perfectly good sense until we consider the educational issues that come into play with large class sizes. There are good reasons why most teachers want reasonably sized classes. Educational psychology suggests large class sizes are less educationally sound. Educational research demonstrates several improvements in academic and non-academic domains associated with reduced class sizes, including student motivation and achievement, parental involvement, and teacher attrition. Even better, such improvements usually seem more pronounced with economically disadvantaged and/or minority students.[1] Yet, the music education profession remains focused on classes with larger enrollments. This is rarely (if ever) the case for other subjects. A math teacher would probably do more than just complain if told there would be 80 students in an algebra class. I think that teacher would make the case that 80 students is more like three or four classes rather than one.

Is it possible we are more concerned with group outcomes than we are about the individuals that make up the group? It appears that large performing groups are too often not about the individual learning, but instead, more about the sum of the parts (students). For example, concerts, festivals, and contests, the most often celebrated goals of ensembles, usually serve as benchmarks for how well parts function as a group, and not as a measure of individual accomplishment. When a high school orchestra performs at a festival, all the students in the ensemble receive the same score. Such a measurement of success would rarely (if ever) be accepted in other academic settings. Could you imagine a math teacher grading a final exam and proudly announcing that the class scored a 92? Obviously, every student in the class didn't score a 92, but that point is masked when a single score represents the entire group of students as one. Since the class scored a 92, everyone gets an "A" for a final grade. Doesn't matter that some students in the class learned very little. Unfortunately, it is the same with ensembles. The string orchestra that scores a "first division" rating at a festival contains some students that are very strong players. However, it probably also involves students that can't read the music in front of them and "fake it" more than actually playing. Then, no doubt, there are a good number of average students – some a little above average, and some a little below. But none of this matters as long as the ensemble gets the "superior" rating. The school principal is happy, the parents are happy, and as a result, the ensemble director is happy. Then it's time to start rehearsing for the next concert and the pattern repeats itself. When class size is too large there simply isn't enough time to devote to individual students, especially those that are struggling.

More than 30 states have limitations on class sizes in one form or another. In 2003, in an attempt to improve student performance, Florida set a limit of 22 students in middle school classes, and 25 in high school classes. By the way, the statute is entitled "An act relating to quality education." A quality education, in this example, is related to smaller class size. However, the Florida Music Education Association (FMEA) was successful in making sure music classes were exempt from this legislation. There are a couple of negative repercussions from this action. First, what does it say about our interest in student learning and achievement? It could certainly be assumed by anyone, with more than a casual interest, that making sure each and every student reaches their maximum potential is not our main objective. I doubt there are music teachers that would say they weren't interested in helping students individually, but our actions speak louder than our words. Second, the wording of the Florida legislation explicitly states that the class size issue is for "core curricula classes." The list of core areas includes Language Arts/Reading, Mathematics, Science, Social Studies, Foreign Languages, Self-Contained (e.g., kindergarten, first grade), Exceptional Student Education, and English for Speakers of Other Languages (ESOL). Here is a case where the music education profession actually chose not to be considered part of the educational "core." The legislation states very clearly that courses outside the core curriculum, such as physical education classes and fine arts classes, are not included. The exact language refers to these courses as "extracurricular." This is not a classification for which we should be striving.

Twenty students in a high school math class is almost always better than 50. An 80-member musical ensemble might look good from an advocacy standpoint, but not from an educational perspective. *It is essential that different types of music classes (beyond band/choir/orchestra) allow for reasonable class sizes equivalent to other academic areas.* The issue we face is creating demand for a sizable total enrollment in music courses, but this enrollment doesn't have to be in one class. In Chapter 5 we will look at some possibilities that work well within the context of reasonable class sizes.

2) *Student Autonomy.* By the early nineteenth century it was common for conductors, who did not also play an instrument during performance, to lead ensembles. Their primary roles were to set tempi, communicate beat and unify the performers. Richard Wagner is credited in large part with re-shaping the conductor's role by adding musical interpretation of music to their duties. By the time choral music entered the public schools in the United States, the conductor, or choirmaster in this case, had become the exclusive leader of the ensemble. It was this person who would normally control all aspects of the ensemble. This was the model used, as well, for instrumental ensembles when they entered schools later. As was the case in other school courses at the time, the adult teacher was the person in control of learning in the classroom. In this design of education, the teacher determines what will be taught, how it will be taught, and how it will be assessed. The teacher is at the center of attention. A student's role is to soak in the knowledge being provided by the teacher. This is the design that continues to drive the greater majority of music education classrooms today, especially in secondary schools.

There are fairly obvious reasons why this model has been helpful with traditional music performance ensembles, and of course ensemble size plays a role here. The larger the ensemble, the more difficult it becomes handing over control to students. A typical concern with allowing students control in a music performance setting is that it would be time consuming and would result in less time for actual music making. And that's the key issue that tends to keep the traditional model so pervasive. With the profession being so dominated by performance, anything that might place limits on the quantity and quality of performance is typically seen as detrimental to student learning. However, questions remain concerning exactly what students are, or are not, learning in such teacher-centered models.

Several developments in education have challenged traditional ways of thinking about classroom learning. Based in large part on work by John Dewey (1859–1952), Jean Piaget (1896–1980), and Jerome Bruner (b. 1915), learning theories such as constructivism and inquiry-based learning call for a much more active role for students.[2] In such models, the center of attention shifts from the teacher to the student. Instead of solely taking in what they are told, students are given freedom to come up with solutions to problems and questions. This forces students to search for information and to learn on their own with direct guidance from the teacher. It also allows for students to make significant use of, and adapt, prior knowledge they bring with them to the classroom. Students, of any age, certainly know a lot about music from their experiences outside of school, but traditional methods of teaching typically do not honor this, nor allow students much opportunity to take advantage of it.

Why should music teachers consider a learner-centered approach? According to Doyle (2011) the answer is simple, "fifteen years of neuroscience, biology and cognitive psychology research findings on how humans learn offer this powerful and singular conclusion: IT IS THE ONE WHO DOES THE WORK WHO DOES THE LEARNING" (p. 2). That is worth saying again. *The one who does the work does the learning.* It is so simple a concept, but traditionally the teacher does much of the musical work. Students tend not to be involved in the real musical work. Instead, they are asked to technically realize the musical learning done by the director. In a primarily learner-centered music class students are tasked with doing much, if not all, the musical work.

Several school music programs do involve students in solo and small ensemble experiences, which can allow individuals and small groups some level of control over their learning. These too often, however, tend to be short-term extensions to the real business of the full ensemble, and often fall short of providing adequate exposure to learner-centered involvement to make much of a difference. Experience once or twice a year isn't sufficient. Instead, it takes sustained involvement for significant results.

Pause for Reflection

With what types of musical work might students be tasked in a music performance class outside the band/choir/orchestra tradition?

In her landmark study on informal learning in the music classroom. Lucy Green (2008) examined the effects of allowing students total autonomy over what they do in music classes. This included choice of music they would study, the instruments they would use, and the methods by which they would learn it, including pace and structure. She discovered that, 1) students tended to make music for longer periods of time and experienced what Csikszentmihalyi[3] called "flow"; to a greater extent, 2) students achieved "flow" in part because they were relieved from the teacher demand to "get it right"; 3) students valued "having to work things out for themselves"; 4) learner autonomy lead to a better sense of satisfaction with learning, resulting in a positive impact on self-confidence; 5) teachers felt students learned more than when involved with "normal" music lessons, displayed increased personal creativity, produced more musically interesting and sophisticated compositions, demonstrated increased motivation, and were more involved in musical tasks.

Green suggests that allowing students a significant level of autonomy in their music learning

> is more likely to foster a celebratory relationship with the music, increasing motivation, opening ears, and ultimately allowing pupils to access the music more deeply, not only in relation to its delineations, but at the inter-sonic level. It also connects again, with imaginative play, without which, musical experience would be impoverished.
>
> (Green 2008, p. 116)

She concludes that "Through adopting and adapting such learning practices in the classroom, not as a substitute, but as a complement to more formal teaching methods, we are making the autonomy of the learner into a means to becoming educated, not necessarily an end of education" (p. 117).

Linnenbrink-Garcia, Maehr, and Pintrich (2011) cite work from Decia and Porac (1978) that investigates links between student autonomy and intrinsic motivation, suggesting that,

> When students are intrinsically motivated, they are more likely to seek out and master challenges, which satisfy their needs to be competent and self-determining ... Intrinsic motivation will suffer when individuals cannot exercise self-determination. They want to feel responsible for their actions and free to make choices. Unfortunately, in many classrooms, students have few choices about what to do and when and how to do it.
>
> (Linnenbrink-Garcia, Maehr, and Pintrich 1978, p. 242)

In schools where the main goal should be student learning, our traditional teacher-centered model by itself may no longer be credible. While a teacher-centered design can be important in the large ensemble model, it is not necessarily conducive for the most effective student learning. Woodford (1997) suggests we fail to "engage students in those kinds of discourses and creative activities that contribute significantly to the construction of their individualized musical selves" (p. 16). Peters (2004) adds:

> In our narrow practice of emphasizing rote learning, performance over composition, and the development of basic musical skills unconnected to real music practice, we fail to ... [develop] genuine musical understanding. Students leave our classrooms not really knowing what all that music was really for. And after all, what is the point of knowing various conceptual elements of music and not being able to use them.
>
> (Peters 2004, p. 9)

Different types of music classes (beyond band/choir/orchestra) should allow significant student autonomy within the educational environment by enabling students to experience self-directed learning, peer-directed learning, and small group learning in which they control the environment.

Pause for Reflection

Consider the classes in which you are presently enrolled. How might your experience change if you were allowed autonomy in deciding what would be learned?

3) *Musical/Creative Decisions.* In addition to control of the learning environment, the teacher in the large ensemble model is likely making practically all the musical and creative decisions for students. In this educational design, students are often the technicians, carrying out the creative wishes of their music teacher. This is, in fact, what our profession has become most efficient doing – developing performers capable of carrying out someone else's artistic decisions. That sounds pretty harsh doesn't it? And it is! Students who enroll in a music class deserve more.

We arrange our students so that sounds they make center on the director. Then we describe what we want them to do, and we point out aspects in their work that need to be corrected so they will have it right. This description sounds too much like a math class. It removes the creative aspect of music from the grasp of the student and they miss out on the most important facet of our art form. O'Toole (2000) reports, "We often hear music teachers say they desire students to become creative, independent musicians [however] teachers rarely reward students for initiative that deviates from the teachers' educated musical interpretation" (p. 34). This is so even with the presence of National Standards. The new 2014 Standards emphasize conceptual understanding of creating right along with performing and responding. Providing students with significant opportunities making creative decisions with sound still remains challenging for music educators to include in their programs. This is especially true for the traditional performance ensembles. And yet, our profession has been talking about the importance of students as creative agents, at least since the mid-1960s through the MMCP (see Chapter 2), and findings demonstrate the importance of this work regarding the development of students' musical understanding.[4]

There are examples of music teachers becoming inspired and making efforts to give students opportunities to be creative. An orchestra teacher might ask the cellos for an idea of how to phrase a section of music. They might try a couple of ideas out, and the teacher might then ask which the students think is best. While it's a great start, it simply isn't enough. Students will not develop creative skills with a hit-and-miss approach. Understanding creativity is similar to understanding any skill. If you only practice scales once every so often, you will probably not become functional with them. If creative experiences are not done in some systematic, sustained way, chances are most students will not develop a comfort level with creativity. It's quite possible that our traditional ensembles (in their current form) are not adequate models for the development of musical creativity. Hebert (2009) suggests: "the kinds of musicianship, values, and judgments that I have argued should be at the core of a comprehensive music education are difficult, perhaps impossible, to adequately address in traditional large ensembles. Such ensembles clearly offer few opportunities for individual judgments and musical independence" (p. 51).

Can you appreciate how class size, student autonomy, and creative decision making are all tied together? There are good reasons why we traditionally do as we have done. If the class size is too large, allowing students autonomy over their learning is time consuming and burdensome, and giving students license to make creative decisions might hinder the overall progress toward concert preparedness. While control of creative decision making is important for the large ensemble director, *different types of music classes (beyond band/choir/orchestra) would benefit from allowing students to learn from their own creative decisions.* Additionally, students would profit from participation in classes where creative decision making plays a much more important role in the process of learning, where composing/arranging/improvising/song-writing are at least as important as performing and listening.[5,6]

4) *Formal Concerts.* Following the professional model, the primary focus for school ensembles tends to be on public performance. These are prone to be formal concerts which normally, with a couple obvious exceptions, have several characteristics in common. They are planned well in advance. They are advertised. There is a printed program. The ensemble dresses in a uniform of some type. The audience sits quietly during the performance. The members of the ensemble have little to no interaction with the audience during the performance. In most settings, movement from performers and audience members is discouraged. The audience is welcomed, however, to politely applaud after a piece is completed (but not between movements please!) even though most members of the audience didn't understand much of what they just heard, nor enjoyed it considerably (we will address this later). In this environment, the "sound" is considered more important than any other aspect of the musical experience, to the point where both the musicians and the audience are encouraged, or even required, to focus solely on the music itself.

Outside the schools, there are few musical experiences that look like this in our society today. In fact, it is important to understand that in the vast majority of musical cultures in the world, music is more than simply an auditory event. Various attributes, such as movement, dancing, lighting, visual effects, socializing, interaction amid musicians, and between the audience and the musicians, are fundamental and integrated aspects of the musical experience. Music is more than simply the sounds of the instruments used in the performance. School-aged students, and almost everyone in our society for that matter, feel out of place in the formal concert. It is simply a foreign (and uncomfortable) experience for most people. Roger Johnson suggests:

At this point, our educational models and practices represent a bizarre misfit with the contemporary world that would be impossible to imagine in virtually any other field. As a comparison, in a previous article I have suggested that this situation would be "as if the great majority of biology departments were just beginning to notice Darwin and had refused to even acknowledge the possibility of, say, genetics ... By this I mean that [we] are practicing and teaching musical understandings and skills that are self-contained, useful only within a very limited and now largely historic repertory, and are mostly inapplicable and even counterproductive for present musical applications and understandings.

(Johnson 2009, p. 18)

With the formal performance model, the educational goal for school ensembles becomes performing an outstanding concert or obtaining an exceptional rating at a contest. As we've already discussed, in this model the group result takes precedence over individual needs, and the evaluation of individuals is usually reduced to whether or not students can perform their part (or if they show up for the concert). The assumption that musical learning takes place through large group concert preparation is not well documented. When the measure of success remains at the group level there is no assurance that individuals within the group are developing musically. In fact, we know some students simply do not make significant progress, and that many end their public school music experience without adequate musical understanding to independently make music on their own.

When they become the educational goal, concerts tend to dictate most decisions that affect students. What, and how much, can be accomplished during a given rehearsal normally depends on the date of the next concert. As a concert performance gets closer it is not uncommon for minor (or major) panic to set in to make sure all the music is adequately rehearsed. Just as increasing size of ensembles is often a badge of pride for many music teachers, so is increasing the number of concerts. However, more concerts during the school year usually equates to less time for any activities outside of concert music preparation. Increasing the difficulty level of music performed is also usually seen as improvement. Most often this too leads to increased attention on large group rehearsal. Bigger ensembles, more concerts, with more difficult music – these become the goals, and often these lead to more and more class time filled with making sure notes and rhythms are correct. Concern for the development of individual musicianship gets less and less attention.

Because there is invariably "a next concert" there is seldom time for anything that isn't directly related to preparation for it. Even more unfortunate, formal concert preparation too often takes the form of making sure notes, rhythms, and dynamics are correct. Additional aspects of musicality are too frequently neglected. You may have been in an ensemble where the director proclaimed something like, "The concert is two days away and we haven't run straight through this piece yet." This is not the best situation for learning. Too often students are left with fond memories of concerts and contest participation, but little musical understanding that equates to lifelong musical meaning. *Different types of music classes (beyond band/choir/orchestra) need to focus on individual student musical understanding where formal, public performance is significantly reduced, often replaced with a variety of methods where classroom activities can be shared with others in more meaningful ways.*

Pause for Reflection

For music classes outside the band/choir/orchestra tradition, what are some possible alternatives to formal concerts, where students can share "classroom activities" with others?

---

5) *Instruments.* Our traditional way of doing music in the schools typically involves large groups of students, in teacher-centered learning environments, where the teacher makes musical decisions for the students, and the end result is a formal concert. With few exceptions we also tend to focus on a particular group of instruments and use of voices that, again, has a very long history. School instrumental ensembles have employed the same instruments for well over 100 years, and the choral singing model has remained intact over the same amount of time. The string and wind instruments used in school ensembles, and this particular style of singing, were quite fashionable both in society and in popular culture at the start of the twentieth century.

Hymn singing, singing schools, singing clubs, and choral societies had made choral music very popular in the United States. However, several innovations during the late nineteenth and early twentieth centuries helped various styles of singing begin to overshadow choral music. The most significant was probably the establishment of the popular music industry which helped give currency to song singing with instrumental accompaniment. An early aspect of this industry was making available inexpensive sheet music versions of songs. This made it possible for music to be distributed to a wide audience of amateur music makers, who could now sing and play popular songs at home. The advent of the player piano and recording devices such as the phonograph allowed the public to further experience popular song singing in the early 1900s. Finally, the radio and sound films (talkies) helped spread popular song singing to a wider audience. The rise of American popular song drastically changed the musical culture in the United States by the 1940s.

The 1960s witnessed more significant changes to music. New instruments began to appear, and some older instruments underwent development. The guitar become the electric guitar, and electronic organs were popular within several styles of music. Voice amplification became increasingly important, and the microphone would change vocal technique in several ways. Instead of playing featured roles, traditional wind and string instruments began to move to the background. The 1980s brought more changes and more new instruments including those that could synthesize sounds. By the start of the 1990s traditional wind and string instruments had all but disappeared from popular music recordings. Some of the traditional "sounds" remained, but these were more often being performed on new instruments such as sound samplers that, instead of generating sounds as did synthesizers, used recordings of sounds (samples) that were played back usually through the use of a keyboard. Today, digital instruments add a staggering variety of new sounds and sources. Singing has also undergone several alterations with the addition of new vocal styles, including rap, and through advances in new technologies that allow changes to the sound of the human voice.

Before we go further, we need to address a common misconception about the term "instrument." Many people in our profession consider "traditional" instruments as "real instruments." After all, flutes, trumpets, and violins have been around a long time and they've proven themselves. Too often then, newer electronic and digital devices are not considered to be on the same level (I asked you a question related to this in Chapter 1). These are usually thought of as "like" musical instruments, or "fake" instruments – just not the "real" thing. This is a dangerous road to go down for our profession. It basically asserts that what we have historically made music on are real instruments, but these new things that other people use are somehow not as worthy. If we wish to create a wider divide between ourselves and our society, then this attitude should help!

The reality is, there are no "fake" instruments. When used to make music, most anything can be a musical instrument. Let's compare an oboe to an iPad, for example. Both are music instruments when used to make music. They are amazingly quite similar. What will an oboe do if you set it on a table and stare at it? Nothing. What will an iPad do if you set it on a table and stare at it? Nothing. In both cases, what is required in order for music to be produced? Give up? It's a human. That, by the way, is what all musical instruments have in common. A human has to do something. It might be blow in it, hit it, pull a bow across it, strum it, or touch it. But the "instrument" won't make music until a human gets involved. The instrument, in fact, is nothing more than a tool the human uses to produce music. When you come down to it, it isn't really about the instrument – it's about the human and what he/she does with it. But there are more similarities. We all know beautiful music can be produced using an oboe. However, we have all probably also experienced really frightful sounds coming from an oboe. Some of my worst musical nightmares have involved oboe players. Again, it's not about the instrument – it's about the human and what he/she does. So how about the iPad? Stunningly magnificent sounds can be produced on an iPad. There are literally hundreds of music performance apps that, in the hands of the right person, can generate wonderful music. But just as with the oboe, it's also possible to make awful noise, and no one really wants to listen to a bad oboe player or a bad iPad player. The oboe and iPad, when used to make music, are both musical instruments – *real* musical instruments.

There are at least four other similarities between an oboe and an iPad (or any musical instruments for that matter). First, each instrument requires the development of certain performance techniques. There are hand positions to learn, specific finger movements to master, and embouchure difficulties to overcome. Every musical instrument requires the performer to master techniques in order to produce the proper characteristic sounds. Second, there is really only one way to develop these required techniques – practice. It takes practice to master performance skills on both an oboe and an iPad, as well as on any musical instrument. I've personally played both oboes and iPads, and I assure you, each has definite sets of technical demands, and some measure of competency must be obtained with either instrument in order to perform on it well. Remember, it's about the human! Third, the development of musicality is equally as important for both oboists and iPadists. As musical understanding develops, performance on any instrument can be enhanced. Again, the level of musicality displayed in a performance has little to do with the particular instrument being used – making music is about the human interaction with a musical instrument. It is no different on an oboe or an iPad. Finally, no matter how amazing a particular musical instrument is, there are limitations on what a human can do with it. This is true for the oboe, the iPad, and all other musical instruments.

Just because it is "new" or "different" from traditional instruments doesn't make an instrument any less of an instrument. The iPad (or a computer, or a digital synth, or a microphone, or a drum pad) is a real musical instrument – no different than an oboe or a trumpet or a violin.

While not all "new" musical instruments developed, or adapted, in the past 50 years have to do with electronic or digital technology, many do. Most of these instruments have not found their ways into school music education programs in any substantial ways. Roger Johnson (2009) reflects on this issue as another that separates music education from the musical world to which students can relate:

> Music has been one of the media arts since the inception of ampli-
> fication, recording, and broadcasting. Magnetic tape first emerged
> just after World War II and began to be used not just to document
> performances but as a creative medium in itself, like film, through
> editing and multitrack recording. Analog technologies – electronic
> instruments, synthesizers, and effects processors – evolved through
> the 1960s and 1970s and were then followed by the rapid expan-
> sion of digital technologies and media. Throughout this entire
> era, music has been one of the pioneering forms of engagement
> with technology and still remains in its vanguard. Contemporary
> music and musicianship are totally synonymous with technology,
> that is, fully obvious, at least to every person in the developed
> world under about age 40. Needless to say, technology is com-
> pletely integrated within all aspects of music making, performing,
> listening, producing, documenting, distributing, selling, communi-
> cating, and exchanging. Most music recordings, including those of
> classical music, are no longer documents of performances; they are
> performances themselves. This is a critical difference; these tech-
> nologies and media can't be separated or fragmented from musical
> praxis, nor should they be excluded from education.
>
> (Johnson 2009, p. 24)

We should probably also give some thought to another issue regarding musical instruments. We have several examples in history where fashionable musical instruments basically disappeared. Did you realize at one time the lute was extremely popular across much of Europe? There were innumerable lutenists, many composers wrote lute music, it was a common continuo instrument, and the use of the lute to accompany singing was quite popular. The lute was a big deal in musical settings in Europe. But things changed. Composers became interested in other instruments after they exhausted the practical limitations of the lute. Keyboard instruments were used more often to realize a continuo part, and also came to be used for accompaniment. By the 1800s the lute had all but vanished. Today, lutes can be found primarily in two places – large university school of music programs that offer early music ensembles, such as a Collegium Musicum (usually led by a faculty member with a title containing the term "historian"), and museums. Sure there are still people who play the lute, but they are anything but common. The lute has fallen out of favor and is no longer important in society. It's natural – new things come and old things go. The harpsichord was once very important in musical society. It helped replace the lute. But the piano helped replace it.

What does the disappearance of the lute, or the harpsichord, have to do with instruments we use in music classes today? After all, the model of music education in the United States was never based around the lute. Well, I don't know if you've noticed, but you are living during a period of great change in musical instruments. Today, new things are coming and old things are going. The last 60 years has witnessed amazing new developments in musical instruments, and at the same time, many traditional instruments have begun (or continued) to disappear. Let's take a look at a couple of examples. During the 1930s and 1940s swing music was all the rage. The clarinet was a very popular instrument and played prominent roles in most big bands of the time. Several acclaimed band leaders, including Benny Goodman, Artie Shaw and Woody Herman, were clarinetists. Everyone knew their names. There were steady jobs for clarinet players who were able to make a good living as performers. Playing a clarinet was cool. It would be normal for a student entering middle school (probably junior high school then) during this time to know Benny Goodman, and his music. Lots of middle school students wanted to be just like Benny Goodman and I'm sure they were quite excited when they discovered they could learn to play the clarinet in school. But time has changed all this. The clarinet has faded away in our society. If shown a picture of a clarinet today, many students wouldn't be able to identify it, let alone name a professional who plays it. The clarinet is no longer cool for many people.

For another example I want to quote Libby Larson. Libby is a real, live, Grammy Award-winning composer. She is perhaps one of the most performed American composers living. In 1997, she presented the plenary address to the National Association of Schools of Music Conference. In that address she considered this idea of instruments dying away and used The Tonight Show Band as a case in point. She said,

> In the mid-1950's Steve Allen hosted the Tonight Show. He performed his own music on the grand piano, which was situated front and center. When Skitch Henderson took over as the director of The Tonight Show Band, he played the piano, and conducted the band. The band was made up of brasses, woodwinds, a few strings, and drum set. The grand piano was still located front and center. When Doc Severenson took over the job of music director from Skitch Henderson, Doc played the trumpet, and the grand piano was moved slightly off to the right-but still in front. Then Branford Marsalis took over as director. He played saxophone, and the piano was moved much further to the right. A synthesizer was added to the

piano, and the keyboard sound was more synthesized than acoustic. Note also that the term "piano" was replaced by "keyboards." Kevin Eubanks took over for Branford Marsalis. His instrument is the electric guitar. The piano has disappeared. Now there are only electric keyboards, and they are placed out of sight.[7]

Was Libby Larson suggesting the piano is dying away and being replaced by other instruments? How can that be? After all, isn't the piano a permanent musical fixture? Won't there *always* be pianos? Won't there always be clarinets? Well, always is a long time, and none of us know the answer to those questions, but certainly you are living during a period of great change in musical instruments. Today, new things are coming and old things are going. The clarinet, oboe, flute, violin, trumpet, tuba, and yes, the piano, have been marginalized in our culture. Their places are being taken by other instruments – some old, some new. Will there always be pianos? Will there always be clarinets? Probably so. After all, we still have lutes and lute players. But if that's your only concern, you are missing the point. The lute is no longer culturally relevant, and we are fast approaching the time, if we aren't already there, when several other traditional musical instruments will join the lute.

I'm guessing this may be very hard for you to accept. It really hits home when you consider the possibility that the instrument you play, your musical joy, could be culturally irrelevant. You probably have spent a good percentage of your life learning to play an instrument. You've most likely spent a lot of money learning to play an instrument. You have, no doubt, spent countless nights working on difficult sections of music, all for the love of playing your instrument. And I bet you are thinking, "That certainly can't be going away!" Yet, you probably don't have nearly as hard a time accepting the demise of the lute. I would guess there was once a lot of lute players that felt the same way you do now. They believed the lute couldn't possibly be replaced by something else. They believed the lute would always be culturally relevant. They were wrong, and so are you if you really believe things aren't changing. I'm going to ask you a question again that I asked at the beginning of this chapter. Should our goal be to perpetuate the type of musical experience we enjoyed as students, or should we adapt as necessary to reach new generations with musical experiences that might be more meaningful and relevant to them? Again, this is a most important question. Students gain personal satisfaction and meaning from performing instruments that appeal and intrigue them, and *different types of music classes (beyond band/choir/orchestra) must make use of newer technologies and instruments that are of interest to, and chosen by students (student autonomy) and are part of the culture in which they live.*

Pause for Reflection

Which musical instruments do you think have been the most popular in the United States over the past several years? Is there a change in this trend right now? Go to the iTunes top ten songs today and see if you notice something these songs have in common.

---

6) *Musical Styles and Ensembles.* Our present-day school ensembles were well established by the 1920s. Up to this time, the music they performed was a significant part of the musical society. As we well know, this is no longer true. Today, much of the music performed by school ensembles has become so esoteric that perhaps the only way to categorize it is "school music." Little of this music has relevance to the lives of students outside of school, and few students find it meaningful even in school. The issue here is closely related to both instruments and ensemble type. As we just discussed, the instruments, and singing styles, we use in our school music models were once quite popular. Today they exist, at best, on the fringes of our culture. The schools are, in fact, the last significant setting for most of the traditional wind and string instruments. Our traditional ensemble model, with uniformed members, led by a conductor, was also fashionable at the beginning of the nineteenth century. But here again, this musical setting and the musical styles it includes exists only on the periphery of our culture today. The music education profession's declaration of "music for all students" rings hollow when our real objective is to forward our legacy of musical traditions. Marie McCarthy (2009) suggests our goal should instead be to better relate to our present society.

> The goal of attuning music in education to music in society at large is both grand in scope and powerful in consequence. The roots of school music traditions are often disconnected from the dynamic sociocultural force we call "music"; they can be revitalized by drawing on the wellsprings of music in the daily lives of students, teachers, and communities, from local to global.
>
> (McCarthy 2009, p. 36)

I believe it is easy for those of us in the profession to be misled. We tend to be so engrossed in our model of music making that we become convinced those outside our profession delight in concert bands, choirs, and orchestras just as we do. But few do. Only in very rare cases are school music concerts attended by many that are not family or friends of the performers. A large number of audience members do not attend our concerts for the music, but rather as supporters of individual students. There are few people, from our general society, who have much interest in what we do. It isn't that they don't value music and musical performances. They don't value the music making we do in schools. Thomas Regelski (2009) suggests,

> Clearly, then, music *is* highly valued by society. So the value of *music* is not the issue ... No, it is *music education – school* music – that is the problem. School music has become its own institution, its own limited kind of musicking. However, since it is not widely seen as relevant to the music world outside of school, it comes under suspicion – all the more so as schooling in general is increasingly pressured to produce results that make noteworthy differences for individuals and society.
>
> (Regelski 2009, p. 190)

The issue at the heart of the matter is musical style. The styles of music that best fit our ensembles, just like many of the instruments we employ in them, are no longer culturally relevant. This is not a new problem. It was recognized, by leaders in our own profession, in the 1960s. Music educators at the 1967 Tanglewood Symposium agreed that "Music of all periods, styles, forms, and cultures belong in the curriculum. The musical repertory should be expanded to involve music of our time in its rich variety, including currently popular teen age music and avant-garde music, American folk music, and the music of other cultures."

Now, I have to tell you, the 1960s happened a very long time ago. If you weren't alive then you can't be expected to fully grasp this, but 50-plus years is a very long time. After all this time why are we still struggling with the issue of musical styles in music education? It is because the instruments we use, and the types of ensembles we employ, fit naturally with certain styles of music. Similarly, they do not easily accommodate other musical styles. It isn't that we haven't heeded the Tanglewood recommendations. In fact, many within the profession today would agree that expanding to include various musical styles is very important. The problem is we have mainly tried to achieve this by incorporating others musics within our model of traditional ensembles, and the results are usually unsatisfactory.

There's just something inauthentic about a Bob Dylan folk song being performed on clarinets and trumpets, or a Green Day piece performed by a concert choir, or an African sega dance song played by a string orchestra. It is ironic that musicians who normally stress authentic performance practice, such as the correct direction for a Baroque mordent, aren't bothered by such arrangements. Normally the composer's intent receives the utmost reverence, but we don't seem to be as concerned about music from other musical styles. Such attempts to expand the musical repertory of our classrooms are not working. Students know the difference. The student who has the entire collection of Beatles tunes on his phone probably isn't interested in the symphonic band arrangement of "Music of the Beatles" published by Hal Leonard. This piece of music, however well done, is not an accurate depiction of the particular musical style it is meant to represent. We can do better. We must do better.

In order to attract interest in music education programs, different types of music classes (beyond band/choir/orchestra) must include a variety of musical styles and genres, and should embrace popular styles, including cultural/ethnic considerations of interest to, and chosen by students (student autonomy). Many of these musical styles come with authentic learning and performance practices that are not well suited to our traditional ensembles. Instruments, ensembles, and musical styles are all closely related. In order to expand the musical repertory of music education, as suggested at the Tanglewood Symposium, we need to expand to include instruments well beyond the traditional wind and string instruments, and music groupings well beyond our traditional ensembles. Some schools might find an Afro-Cuban music ensemble of great interest to students, while others could have success with ensembles based on Latin or Asian musics. Students at many schools could benefit from courses dealing with different popular music styles found in the United States such as rock, pop, country, or rap, and probably any school would be successful offering digitally based music classes that involved production and recording. All such new courses require the music education profession to move outside our traditional comfort zone and embrace new instruments and ensembles in our programs.

Pause for Reflection

What musical styles are on your music listening device? What percentage of your music library are in the different styles represented on your device? What do you think you would find if you asked "typical" middle school students these questions?

---

7) *Traditional Notation.* Our traditional ensembles are bound to standard music notation out of necessity, as rote learning in large groups is typically tedious and can slow learning to a crawl. Since these ensembles have dominated music education in the United States, the

ability to read and write music is seen as being of the utmost importance. However, is learning to read and write musical notation essential, or even beneficial in all school music settings? When I hear my college students talk about teaching the "basics" of music they are usually talking about reading and writing quarter notes. We have fooled ourselves into believing that students *must* learn notational skills in order to develop musically. Because of this, teaching these skills is prominent at all levels of K-12 music education. Starting in primary grades, students are normally introduced to the staff, clefs, and basic rhythm durations like quarter notes and rests. They are taught words like "piano," "forte," "andante," and "allegro." This continues in a progressive manner until students are "ready" to join traditional ensembles. Students enrolled in secondary school ensembles then continue to develop their understanding of notational skills through their ensemble participation.

There are some issues with this system to which we should give thought. First, because of the significance placed on reading and writing music notation, it is easy to get the impression these are fundamental and essential to understanding music. This is, however, far from the truth. Music is an aural art. Understanding music, and I mean getting to the essence, the significance of music, has to do with making sense of sound – not written symbols. Our notation system is a language. As with all languages, the main goal is to communicate specific messages. In music, communication through notation is typically between composers and performers. The composer needs to communicate specific pitches, played for specific lengths of time, by specific instruments, in specific ways. In certain musical styles, especially those based on Western European classical traditions, this communication is absolutely necessary. However, even in these styles, this written language is not the *music*. The music is what results from this communication, aided by the knowledge, craftsmanship, understanding, sensitivities, and artistries of the performer. Music is the sound. The meaning of music is found principally by exploring the sound, and not through the written symbols of notation. We do a disservice to students when we so overemphasize the written aspects of music that they begin to see notation as fundamental to understanding what music is about.

Second, are you aware that a vast majority of musical styles throughout history have never been notated? You probably know quite a lot about a couple of these. Most jazz and rock styles are traditionally not notated. These musics are normally passed on through aural transmission, where the performers build skills with their ears, instead of their eyes. Chances are you know musicians who don't read or write music notation. Some of the most exceptional musicians I've worked with didn't read. One of the more disturbing musical experiences I've had involved a setting where several jazz players, from different parts of the country, were brought to a high school jazz festival to be clinicians and judges. They were also asked to perform an evening concert as a combo. The evening before the concert they met to rehearse. It was the only rehearsal time they would have. During the first 15 minutes or so they exchanged stories about people (cats) they had played with. Then, with a little prompting, the rehearsal began. One player suggested a tune they might play. There was general agreement that this tune would be fine. Another tune was suggested with the same result. This went on until a tune name came up with which one player was unfamiliar. With no hesitation the musician that suggested the tune walked to the piano and plucked out a few chords while singing a melodic line (the head). The player who didn't know the piece then said it was fine, and they went on to other tunes. There was some discussion concerning what key to use on one particular piece, but that was easily resolved. That was it. That was the rehearsal, which by the way, ended when one of the guest musicians said, "When do we eat?" The horn players didn't even open their cases. The next evening, this group of musicians performed an extraordinary 90-minute concert – and there was no printed music to be found.

Why would I call this perhaps the most *disturbing* musical experience I have had? It wasn't because I laid awake for quite awhile that night wondering how we were going to salvage the concert. No, I was disturbed when I realized the music education profession has little regard for this type of musicianship. We might in words, but not in actions – and our actions speak louder than our words. We don't typically train future music teachers to hear music this way – to learn music this way. Why not? Because we are so tied to music notation. We make the notation seem so basic to learning music that we allow it to get in the way of our ears. When notation is the basis for musical understanding, we severely limit the breadth of potential musical encounters for our students. Roger Johnson (2009) suggests such emphasis is "disabling" students:

> This strongly suggests what to most musicians is already obvious: that contemporary musical practice has indeed become vastly more *aural* than visual, more interactive and collaborative than prescribed. Prenotational practices have fused with those of technology, and the need for notation has simply ceased to be nearly as important as it was in the nineteenth and early twentieth centuries. Educationally speaking, too, this development gives clear evidence that much of what is now taught and learned mostly through notation – theory, musicianship, performance skills, and analysis – would be more effectively and productively done primarily aurally and through direct application. No doubt some use

of visual representation would still be useful, but mostly as a way to document what is first heard. However, the limiting and disabling kind of "musical aphasia" caused by over-reliance on notation has no place in musicianship now.

(Johnson 2009, p. 23)

Finally, there is the issue of time. Time is something of which there is usually not enough. This is especially true for music teachers in many elementary schools where instruction can be limited to 45 minutes per week or less. Here's the thing – as we previous discussed, music notation is a language, and with any language, it takes enormous amounts of time and practice to develop functional skills. My wife is a fourth grade classroom teacher where she mainly teaches language arts. She has, on average, ten hours a week to teach reading and writing. In addition to that, her students are given assignments that have them reading and writing at home every day. They need this amount of time and practice in order to make satisfactory progress with language skills. Can you imagine how little improvement her students would make if they were limited to 45 minutes per week of reading and writing instruction, combined with modest to no expectations for home practice? Yet, we make efforts to do just that.

"Some understanding is better than none at all." This is what I hear a lot from music teachers who defend notation instruction even in the face of what is often very limited results. But what is the cost? Are there other musical understandings that could be better developed using the precious limited time that is available? Perhaps a fuller understanding of musicianship, creativity, and aural skills? Development in these areas is compromised when time is taken for traditional notational concepts.

Under what conditions does it make most sense to teach music reading and writing skills? Educational psychologists tell us that students learn best when they are able to practice what they are learning – when they have a practical application of the skills they are being taught. In what setting do students regularly use and practice music notation skills? In what setting do students have a practical application for reading and writing? The most natural setting would probably be the ensembles where reading is required – concert bands, choirs, and orchestras. When students will need and use notation every day is, no doubt, the perfect time to introduce students to reading and writing skills, especially after they have developed aural and creative skills in earlier grades. It doesn't matter, so much, at what grade this begins, just as long as the setting is one where students can make ongoing practical application of what they are learning. This is especially true for language acquisition (again, music notation is a language) – do you know anyone (you perhaps) who endured multiple years of instruction in a foreign language only to lose most of what they learned? Chances are, skills were lost because there was no ongoing practical application. Music notation is a foreign language to students who don't have regular opportunities to practice with it.

There is one more issue we should think about. We know a very low percentage of elementary-aged students will participate in secondary school ensembles that require an understanding of music notation. We also know the greater majority of elementary-aged students will never have any use for music reading and writing skills. Yet we spend (waste) the precious little time we have with them teaching music notation. Perhaps we think if they know how many beats a half note gets, and on what line is the pitch "D," they will want to be a supporter of classical music when they become rich and famous. Maybe instead, using that precious little time we get with students, we might focus on skills that all students will find useful for developing musical understanding. Marie McCarthy (2009) concludes,

> I have identified four traditions that have come to be associated with school music: priority given to musical works, preference for classical repertoire, emphasis on developing performance skills, and commitment to the values and practices of conservatory models of instruction. When students come to view music as synonymous with the notated work, their relationship to music as human expression is reduced and misguided.
>
> (McCarthy 2009, p. 32)

Students involved with musical styles and instruments outside school settings function very well without the need for learning standard notational systems, and these musical involvements often lead to advanced aural skill development. In school-based music education, understanding notation skills is usually considered synonymous with music literacy. Literacy in music, however, has a much different connotation in the greater majority of musical genres throughout the world, and even in traditional forms of American musics including jazz, and rock and roll. *Different types of music classes (beyond band/choir/ orchestra) could benefit from emphasizing aural development over written competence.*

Pause for Reflection

Do you know of people that can play most anything by ear? Have you ever been envious of them? I'm assuming you don't normally play by ear. Why is that?

8) *Lifelong Skills.* One important goal of education should be helping students develop skills and understandings they can make use of throughout life. There is convincing empirical evidence a very large percentage of students that begin participation in secondary school ensembles cease their musical involvements while still in school or soon after leaving high school. Aside from fond memories, there is little indication traditional music education has much of an impact on musical life after high school for most students. Keep in mind that a very small percentage of students even take part in secondary school ensembles. Factor in that few from this small percentage continue their high school musical involvement as adults, and you see the problem. The United States has perhaps the most pervasive school music education system in the world, yet we have very little influence on musical life in our society.

Why is that? A very big part of it has to do with the styles of music we incorporate, the instruments we use, the type of ensembles we employ, and our devotion to written notation. These are no longer a significant part of twenty-first century life in the United States, especially within youth cultures. As a result, only a very low percentage of students opt to be involved with music in the schools past elementary school, and for the few that do, we don't provide them with musical understandings that might allow for independent musicianship when they leave our ensembles. Regelski (2009) suggests,

> Teaching musicianship, then, requires attention to the nature and requirements of the musics at stake – to how, when, where, and under what other conditions in "real life" these musics exist and, thus, to the progressive ability of the student to understand the musical needs and criteria at stake and to make effective choices *independently* of a teacher. Given school circumstances, all that needs to be learned can never be taught; thus learners must be *taught how to learn* on their own.
>
> (Regelski 2009, p. 192)

He continues,

> Such musical independence is more difficult to develop when large ensembles are the sole or major curricular vehicle. An education rich in solos, duets, and various chamber combinations – including the smaller ensembles characteristic of many musics—increases independence. Musicianship that is relevant to several musics – albeit usually in different ways – provides students with more opportunities for different uses that fine tune their skills and abilities. Musical independence is also required for listening, composing, and other musical "doings."
>
> (Regelski 2009, pp. 192–193)

There has also been a lot written lately about participatory music making versus presentational music making.[8] Many of the musical practices in the world are participatory in nature. In these settings the line between audience and artist is blurred and there is active involvement with musical sound by most everyone present. This allows for a wide range of participants, from amateurs to professionals, to be involved in the same experiences. This form of music making tends to be open with varying degrees of, often, repetitive structures. There is normally a high degree of socialization during music making and the beginnings and endings of music are often loose and sometimes disorderly. Often participants can enter and exit music making as they feel comfortable.

On the other hand, the vast majority of our school music-making experiences are presentational in nature. In these settings, the music making is the sole responsibility of the "musicians" present. The audience's only roles are to silently listen, and then politely applaud at the appropriate times. Presentational music making is most often scripted and rehearsed, and tuning and timing are precise.

Many of the musical experiences in current youth culture, in the U.S., contain both participatory and presentational characteristics. In a lot of these settings the audience is actively involved through movement, dance, singing, and socialization. Most school-age students are quite comfortable in these settings and they find these musical experiences meaningful. Not long ago I asked one of our graduate music education students, who was a local high school music teacher, how many of his students came to ensemble performances at our University. He said that he was unaware of any students that attended our concerts – even concerts of the same types of ensembles in which they were participating in high school. I asked if this had to do with cost, as at the time student tickets for our performances were $10 each. He laughed and said it wasn't unusual for his students to pay more than $100 for a ticket to attend a music concert. What do you think his reasoning was for his students' lack of interest in our concerts ...? He said, above all else, they wanted to socialize. Live music for them was more of a participatory event than presentational. Even more important than the music being performed, they (15–18-year-olds) saw musical events as social functions.

This was like a slap in the face for me. What about these students' families? Just like these students, their parents, and grandparents, grew up going to popular music *shows* – musical events that were, in many ways, participatory events. They (15–18-, 35–40-, and 55–65-year-olds!) found meaning in music that was participatory.

These issues may have a lot to do with the difficulty we face convincing those outside the profession of the importance of music study. It isn't necessarily that people feel music in the schools is unimportant – it's that they can't identify with our model of music education that seems to prepare only a select few for professional or semi-professional music making, while ignoring the musical needs of the many. Regelski (2007) adds, "But amateuring should be at the heart of both 'value added' and 'authentic assessment' conceptions of music education. Such rehabilitation of amateuring as a valid and valuable curricular action ideal would do much to overcome the declining support for school music" (p. 39).

Helping students find relevance between music study in school and their musical life outside of school will go a long way in the development of independent musicianship and lifelong learning. One example of how this might work would be through involving students in the production of popular musics in school. Bringing musics into the classroom that interest students would help them connect their school musical experiences with their personal lives. Giving students opportunities to copy music they enjoy, and to create their own music in styles that interest them could very well lead to musical involvements that would continue long after they leave school. However, it is still rare that experiences like this are provided to students in schools. The excuse I often hear is that students already do this outside of school, and our job should be guiding them to new experiences with musical styles with which they are not familiar (translated: ... with musical styles that "I" enjoy, and believe are of greater value).

Regelski (2007), discussing the development of musical amateurs, and the importance of music outside the traditional canon, suggests,

> The traditional premise behind formal music education has therefore been the assumption that the Classical music favored historically by the middle class is inherently good and superior to the popular musics of the underclasses ... Such other musics, from the first decried as déclassé by aristocratic musical patrons, are correspondingly devalued, disregarded, even actively dismissed in schools. The curriculum and performance "programs" of schools (and private studios, as well) have rarely addressed such musics and other forms of musicking.
>
> (Regelski 2007, p. 25)

I find this attitude by music teachers is often rooted in their own lack of willingness to learn. It is far more comfortable teaching within musical styles that interest you, rather than extending yourself to reach students where they are. This "let them come to me" perspective is not working very well. Isn't it possible to start where students are *and* guide them in new directions at the same time? Of course it is. But as with all things involving change, this requires that we give up some comfort and expand our own understandings.

I want to go back to the belief, held by many in our profession, that students already know about popular music and make it on their own outside of school. What exactly do most students "know" about the music that interests them? The average middle school student can probably teach you the words to every song they like. They can sing along with the recordings of an amazing number of songs. They can do a lot of the dance moves they watch on videos. Chances are they follow their favorite artist's personal lives. They know who has been arrested, who is involved with who, and when a concert tour will bring popular acts close enough to attend. All of this is very meaningful to students, and it does demonstrate the importance of music in their lives, however, from a musical standpoint most school-aged students have a very limited understanding of any music. Green (2008), while having students aurally copying a recording of their own choosing, by ear, discovered,

> there was evidence to suggest that many pupils' ordinary listening stance was indeed, very passive, inattentive or undiscerning ... For many of them revealed, rather implicitly than explicitly, that when they started out on the listening and copying task they could hear little more than either the lyrics or the main vocal melody of the song. Many of them expressed surprise to discover that "there is more to it" than that!
>
> (Green 2008, p. 73)

There is much students can learn about "their" music, and they would find it exciting, motivating, and relevant if we were to help them.

What's more, there are precious few school-aged students who take part in active making music on any regular basis outside of schools. In some of my personal research I have examined how students make music in ensembles they form outside of school. In working with a large number of high schools I've never had difficulty finding such groups (garage bands, hip-hop groups, metal bands, etc.), but I've been amazed by how few students actually participate in these types of active music making. My sense is, there exists a very large population of students who love musics that we typically ignore in the schools, and many of them would be very excited about an opportunity to learn how to perform and create this music in school settings (just as it was in the 1930s when students in schools were excited by the possibility of learning to play the music they liked on the clarinet).

So again I'm going to ask you the question – should your goal be to perpetuate the type of musical experience you enjoyed as a student, or should you adapt as necessary to reach new generations with musical experiences that might be more meaningful and relevant to them? Before we move on, we need to address answers to this question that

I have now asked three times. I suppose there are at least three possible answers. One is, perpetuate. I would suggest this is a dangerous stance as it ignores several realities in which the profession finds itself. You have every right, however, to feel this is the correct answer, but I hope you will remain open to other possibilities. A second answer is, adapt. Obviously I feel this is a worthy answer as it would give the profession added hope in reaching unserved populations with music education in schools. The third possible answer is, both. And I don't doubt that this is a popular answer. Let's hang on to the best of what we do, and add new possibilities to it. Yes, this could be a very good answer. However, it could also be a way of covering up the desire to "perpetuate" while pretending to "adapt." I'm afraid I see this attitude often as I visit K-12 schools. For example, a music teacher who is "adapting" by offering a guitar class alongside several classes of traditional ensembles. But the teacher runs the guitar class as if it were a concert band, instead of approaching it with a more authentic pedagogical model, or worse yet, the teacher spends most of the guitar class in their office allowing the students to do what they want – as long as they behave. From the outside it would appear changes have occurred in the school music program, but in reality very little has changed. If you take the stance that both "perpetuating" and "adapting" are important, you must be willing to give at least the amount of time, interest, and energy to the adapted aspects of a program as the perpetuated. Anything else cheats students.

We know that, in addition to the large percentage of students that stop school music participation after elementary school, too many students leave our programs unprepared to continue their school music experience. *If we expect to be taken seriously as a school subject we must give considerable thought to the enhancement of lifelong musical skills when developing different types of music classes.*

9) *Entry Level.* Most traditional school programs have "beginning" ensembles where students build skills they can use in more advanced classes later. These beginning ensembles most often occur in the late elementary grades and/or in early middle school grades. If a student misses this entry-level experience it is not uncommon for them to find it difficult to enter in later years. Often, serious options for the beginning student are not available if they don't begin a performance program at the normal starting point. I've too often heard stories about students visiting the high school band director saying they enjoyed seeing the band perform and have now decided they would like to join. The band director, with obvious excitement in their voice, inquires about what instrument the student plays. The student responds that they don't play an instrument, but they would like to learn. The band director, excitement now gone from their tone, tells them that if they go get lessons

and come back ready to join, that maybe they could then talk about the possibilities. The student never comes back.

This is certainly not true in all school music settings, but it is almost always an easier road for students who begin school ensemble instruction at the "right" time. While this is typically a more prominent problem in instrumental ensembles, it can also be true for choral groups. We further limit enrollment possibilities for late starters by allowing admission to particular ensembles by audition only, so that music ensemble choices become even fewer. By the way, the physical education people have this one figured out. They offer what we might consider "general physical education" as academic subjects during the school day. Generally all students can enroll in these courses at any grade level and they usually experience a wide range of activities. Previous experience and present skill level do not matter. Select students can then "audition" for specific types of athletic activities that tend to occur after school. If you are good enough you can join the baseball team, but anyone, in any grade, can participate in baseball during school. Perhaps this isn't a bad model for music education, where "general" musical experiences (including performance) are offered for academic credit during school time. Students could join these classes at any point in their school career, and there would be no particular skill levels required. Then "auditioned" performance opportunities would be made available as after school activities for the more proficient students who are interested.

I've seen this work at some schools, but many music teachers I talk with worry that enough students wouldn't dedicate the necessary time after school. They are concerned students would have too many other activities, or they would have to work, or they couldn't find a ride, etc. This is important to think about. There are scores of after school athletic teams, academic clubs, and social organizations that often attract many more students than they need. Why might we have trouble interesting students in our traditional ensembles after school? After all, students who really want to play on the football team figure out ways to fit in the required time and practice. Do you find it worrisome, as I do, that we would have trouble getting this kind of commitment for an extra-curricular music ensemble?

Many of the previous issues we've looked at are involved here. Large class sizes make it difficult for a music teacher to help beginning students in an ensemble setting when they struggle – it is just as easy for the struggling student to "fake it" and hide within the group. The demands of formal concerts make it imperative that students be of a certain ability level for ensemble participation (a chain is only as strong as its weakest link). The types of instruments we use in instrumental ensembles normally require significant time and practice to master, so much so, that students thrown into a setting that is too advanced might become frustrated as they are asked to perform technically beyond their ability. Traditional choral settings, similarly, require the development of vocal technique over time, and it can be very difficult for a beginning singer placed in an advanced choral group. Finally, the demands of traditional notation, for students with little to no previous notation reading experience, can hinder progress in a group where others are much more advanced. Our model of music education makes it difficult for older beginners to participate. This is a serious problem as it discourages older students from beginning music instruction.

Once a student has missed the entry point for participation in traditional ensembles it is often difficult to break into the system as a beginner. Few high school programs (especially instrumental) have *serious* options for students with no previous performance skills. *Different types of music classes (beyond band/choir/orchestra) must not only allow, but encourage students to start music instruction at any grade level, and provide opportunities for them to be placed into small group settings where students of varying abilities and experience can learn with, and from, each other.*

10) *Developing Functionality.* This is directly tied to entry level and life -long skills, but it is a separate issue. In traditional performance programs it normally takes several years of practice and study to achieve a functional level on an instrument (including the voice). Even with a full year of ensemble experience in a band, choral, or string class a student is not likely to have achieved a level of musicianship sufficient to sustain musical activity if they stop their in-school participation. When music teachers think of student participation in ensembles, they desire that students will be involved for four, five, or six years. By their senior year, then, students hopefully will perform at an advanced level. This is the nature of the instruments we employ and the character of typical performance settings for school ensembles.

There are two problems here. First, many students, who are interested in secondary school music ensembles, find it becoming progressively more difficult to maintain music enrollment over several years. Some students are drawn to Advanced Placement courses, International Baccalaureate (IB) programs, college tracks, dual enrollment classes, and other offerings that might help with college admissions and placement. Students tend to have only a limited number of elective slots available to them, and music can be easily squeezed out. Other students are increasingly required to enroll in remedial courses in areas such as reading, writing, and math to help them with mandated testing. There are also students who have several interests and it is difficult for them to devote too many class periods to music. Some states have begun three-year high school programs where students can elect to graduate quicker, in part by taking fewer elective courses. Even for those students who are so inclined, it can be an arduous journey enrolling in a music ensemble over a period of multiple years.

The necessity of taking several years of practice and study to achieve a functional level on an instrument in traditional ensembles is problematic for another group of students – those who will only take the minimum number of arts-related courses. Some students will only enroll in arts courses in order to meet graduation requirements, while others may take one specific music class just for the experience. After elementary school, these students (and there are a lot of them) might be in a music class for as little as one year, or even half a year. In many cases this limited exposure to a traditional ensemble class, especially at a beginning level, will not provide students with a satisfactory musical experience that they will be able to draw on throughout life.

Ideally, different types of music classes (beyond band/choir/orchestra) need to help students reach a functional level of musicality within one year or less, providing students who cannot, or choose not to participate in school music classes for longer periods, the ability to independently enhance their musicality after they leave us.

At the start of this chapter I suggested there are several opportunities for change that are worthy of serious consideration as we look to the future of music education in the United States. I chose the term "opportunities" very carefully. The music education profession is presently, and has been for some time, facing various challenges that may best be dealt with through change. Change can be scary. But change can also be an opportunity. I suggest we are entering a very exciting time for the music education profession as we deal with potential change. I think we have many great opportunities to make music study in the schools as relevant as it has ever been. We also have amazing opportunities to help expand musicianship for all students, and to enhance the musical culture of the United States. The ten opportunities described in this chapter are not meant as an exhaustive list, but certainly provide a good basis from which to begin. None of this will be easily accomplished, but I believe we are up to the challenge.

Pause for Reflection

What other "opportunities" can you think of that I left out?

Notes

1 See *School Class Size: Research and Policy*, ed. by Gene V. Glass, and Tennessee's Class Size Study: Findings, Implications, Misconceptions, by

Jeremy D. Finn and Charles M. Achilles, in *Educational Evaluation and Policy Analysis*, 1999, Vol. 21, no. 2.

2 For excellent source material for constructivism learning theories see: J. S. Bruner (1961). The act of discovery. *Harvard Educational Review* 31 (1): 21–32. Piaget, Jean. (1950). *The Psychology of Intelligence*. New York: Routledge. Dewey, J. (2009). *Democracy and Education: An Introduction to the Philosophy of Education*. New York: WLC Books. (Original work published 1916).

3 See Csikszentmihalyi's books, *Flow: The Psychology of Optimal Experience* (1990), and (1996) *Creativity: Flow and the Psychology of Discovery and Invention* (1996).

4 For example, see, Maud Hickey's *Why and How to Teach Music Composition: A New Horizon for Music Education*, published by MENC in 2003.

5 For an excellent case made for the importance of involving students in creative acts see the College Music Society's November 2014 Task Force Report, "Transforming Music Study from its Foundations: A Manifesto for Progressive Change in the Undergraduate Preparation of Music Majors," at http://myweb.fsu.edu/nrogers/Pedagogy_I/Assignments/CMS_Manifesto.pdf.

6 There is evidence that performance ability developed through comprehensive musicianship models is at least as good, if not better than traditional performance teaching. For example, see James Austin's 1998, *Update* article, "Comprehensive musicianship research: Implications for addressing the National Standards in music ensemble classes."

7 See the full text of Libby Larson's NASM speech at: http://libbylarsen.com/as_the-role-of-the-musician.

8 For an excellent look at participatory vs. presentational music making see Thomas Turino's text *Music as Social Life: The Politics of Participation*, published by University of Chicago Press.

Readings and References

Bartel, L. (2004). *Questioning the Music Education Paradigm*. Volume 2 of Research to Practice, a biennial series. Toronto: Canadian Music Educators Association.

Deci, E. L. and Porac, J. (1978). Cognitive evaluation theory and the study of human motivation. In M. R. Lepper and D. Greene (eds.), *The Hidden Costs of Reward: New Perspectives on the Psychology of Human Motivation*. Hillsdale, NJ: Erlbaum, pp. 149–176.

Doyle, T. (2008). *Helping Students Learn in a Learner-Centered Environment: A Guide to Facilitating Learning in Higher Education*. Sterling, VA: Stylus Pub.

Green, L. (2008). *Music, Informal Learning and the School: A New Classroom Pedagogy*. Surrey, England: Ashgate.

Hebert D. G. (2009). Musicianship, musical identity, and meaning as embodied practice. In Regelski, T. A. and Gates, J. T. (eds.), *Music Education for Changing Times: Guiding Visions for Practice*; Landscapes: the Arts, Aesthetics, and Education series, Volume 7. New York: Springer, pp. 39–58.

Johnson, R. (2009). Critically reflective musicianship. In Regelski, T. A. and Gates, J. T. (eds.), *Music Education for Changing Times: Guiding Visions for*

Practice; Landscapes: the Arts, Aesthetics, and Education series, Volume 7. New York: Springer, pp. 17–28.

Linnenbrink-Garcia L., Maehr, M. L., and Pintrich P. R. (2011). Motivation and achievement. In Colwell, R. and Webster P. R. (eds.), *MENC Handbook of Research on Music Learning: Volume 1: Strategies*. New York: Oxford, pp. 216–264.

McCarthy, M. (2009). Re-thinking "music" in the context of education. In Regelski, T. A. and Gates, J. T. (eds.), *Music Education for Changing Times: Guiding Visions for Practice*; Landscapes: the Arts, Aesthetics, and Education series, Volume 7. New York: Springer, pp. 29–38.

McPherson, G. E. and Hendricks, K. S. (2010). Students' motivation to study music: The United States of America. *Research Studies in Music Education* 32(2): 201–213.

Meyer, D. L. (2009). The poverty of constructivism. *Educational Philosophy and Theory* 41(3): 332–341.

O'Toole, P. (2000). Field report on music in the schools. *Orbit* 31(20): 34–36.

Peters, J. B. (2004). They are not a blank score. In Bartel, L. (ed.), *Questioning the Music Education Paradigm*. Volume 2 of Research to Practice, a biennial series. Canadian Music Educators Association.

Regelski, T. (2007). Amateuring in music and its rivals. *Action, Criticism, and Theory for Music Education* 6(3), http://act.maydaygroup.org/articles/Regelski6_3.pdf.

Regelski, T. (2009). An end is a beginning. In Regelski, T. A. and Gates, J. T. (eds.), *Music Education for Changing Times: Guiding Visions for Practice*; Landscapes: The Arts, Aesthetics, and Education series, Volume 7. New York: Springer, pp. 187–198.

Woodford, P. (1997). Music education, culture and democracy: Sociality and Individuality. *Canadian Music Educator* 39(1): 15–18.

5   Beyond Band, Choir, and Orchestra

In Chapter 4, I introduced several opportunities that are available to the music education profession to improve our situation in schools. Opportunities, that when taken in combinations, could help us realize interesting, relevant, and meaningful musical experiences for students. In this chapter, we will examine some possibilities of what these opportunities could look like in schools. I'll suggest four different settings, but this only scratches the surface. First of all, any of these four could be modified in multiple ways to produce different types of experiences. Then, for every one of these settings there are an untold number of other possibilities. I'm also sure the future will witness yet additional opportunities. As we discussed previously, what works at one school might not work at another school, and what works for one music teacher might not work for another. I hope the settings I present here will help you appreciate some of the possibilities and I trust they will spark additional ideas.

Guitar Class

I'm starting here, for a couple reasons. First, while a guitar class isn't nearly as "traditional" as band, choir, and orchestra, we have experienced a rapid increase of guitar use in the schools during the past decade. We have some history now with teaching guitar in the schools, yet it is still an "outsider" for many music teachers who are not comfortable with the instrument. The amount of guitar instruction in colleges for pre-service music teachers has also grown substantially so that it is no longer uncommon to find course work in music education degree programs that include use of the guitar. So the guitar has begun to enter K-12 music programs, but there is still much that can be accomplished. Second, I worry that in far too many instances the profession has approached the guitar class as if it were another traditional ensemble. Students sit in neat rows or semi-circles, they play out of a book or use sheet music, generally with a good deal of unison playing (several members on a part) and they are "directed" by the teacher. While this model could be successful for guitar instruction, you will be hard pressed to find significant examples of the guitar used this way in our society, especially in youth culture. We have plucked (pun intended) the guitar out of our culture and turned it into a traditional ensemble. It seems we are trying to remove the relevance students might normally feel with this instrument. Why would we do that? Because, the traditional ensemble, conducted by the music teacher, is what we know. It's what we've always done. We sit students in rows and tell them what to do. It's easy, it's efficient, and it's comfortable. And it can make for great concerts. But in this case it's not terribly authentic, and we can do better. Let's look at some possibilities modeled on the opportunities presented in Chapter 4.

Let's start with class size. How many students would be a good fit in a guitar class? I think you would find the answer to that by looking around your school. If math classes and language arts classes have 25 students, then 25 would be a good number of students in a guitar class. If 50 students want to take a guitar class, they should be split up into two classes and not clumped into one. No principal would do that to a math teacher, and we shouldn't let them do it to us. By the way, at what grade level could you have a guitar class? Can middle school students develop a better understanding of music through guitar study? Of course. What about fourth graders? Certainly. What would be the difference between a fourth grade guitar class, and an eighth grade (or twelfth grade) class? One important difference would probably be the pace of learning. Older students would normally bring a wider musical background into the classroom. They would probably have improved fine motor development. More of them might have some previous experience with the guitar. It will probably take more time to make progress with younger students and you have to be ready for that reality. But then again, you might find a particular class of fourth graders that blow past an eighth grade group – it's all part of the challenge of being a teacher. Regardless of the grade level, however, 25 students in a class would be more educationally sound than 50!

Let's look at a possible class setup, and answer a couple basic questions regarding the class. First, what "material" are you going to cover? You could use a published beginning class guitar book.[1] These tend to look a lot like the many beginning band and orchestra series that have been around for years. But instead, let's try a different a more learner-centered approach, and ask the students in the class what they want to learn. Let's find out what they already know about the guitar and what they would like to be able to do with a guitar. Maybe you could start here. Take what they already know, and let where they want to go be a jumping off place for class activities. Certainly, you can expand on their ideas as the class progresses, but beginning with where they are, and taking into account where they would like to go will provide the students with a sense of relevance with the class and should help put them on the road to establishing lifelong musicianship skills. It's quite likely most students in the class would like to learn to play some popular songs, so this might be a very good place to start.

Second, what might a typical class period look like? Let's try to venture away from the traditional ensemble model setup where the teacher has full control over the learning environment. Instead you could place students in small groups (perhaps three to five per group) spaced around the room. Or better yet you might allow students to select their own groups. Each group will serve as both a learner-centered and peer-learning environment and as a small ensemble. Your role now becomes part provider of information and part mentor. You might start by demonstrating an E Major chord to the class and showing them how to hold the left hand, and strum with the right. Charge each group with making sure all its members can play the E Major chord correctly. Allow students in their groups to work on this together as you walk around group to group to check on their progress. At this point, the students actually take over the role of teacher as they help each other play the chord. When you are fairly certain most students have the idea, you could demonstrate a strumming pattern using just the E chord. Again, turn the teaching over to the students and allow them to get their group playing together using this pattern. Depending on the age of the students, as we discussed, this type of an activity could go very quickly, or it might take more time than you would have guessed. Regardless, the goal is to get them playing as soon as possible. Don't get carried away with teaching names of the different guitar parts, all the correct hand positions, posture, and all the other things that tend to bore students when not connected to actual music making. Get them playing first. Part of what you are looking for as you move group to group are chances to demonstrate and teach all these things as you find them necessary.

Pause for Reflection

The idea just presented is frightening for many music teachers. Having students begin making music before they understand correct posture, let alone how to properly hold their instrument, is out of the question. What would be the positive outcomes of getting students playing right away? How would they then fix any technique they have wrong? Why might this method lead to better overall results?

Next, you might be ready with a recording to play, so the class can accompany using their chord and strumming pattern. It doesn't have to be a full song, but maybe a minute of a song. It could be something you created using your digital audio workstation of choice. You want them to feel as if they are really making music. You are spending this time watching individuals and listening. You are learning what you can help students with next. Depending on time, age of students, and all the other things that make teaching a challenge, you want to try and get this far in one class setting if possible, so they leave feeling that they have really done something significant, and that they are capable of playing the guitar. You also want to send them away with homework. Of course, it would be ideal if every student had a guitar at home with which to practice, but this is probably unrealistic. Instead, give them the name of the next chord they need to learn and tell them they need to come to the next class ready to play it. So how are they going to do that? They could get help from a friend or family member that plays some guitar, or most likely they will go to the internet, look up the chord, and listen to it as they watch it being performed. They'll watch and listen and learn. You could even supply them with links to specific web material you want them to experience. You may very well be surprised that, besides what you want them to learn, some students will come to the next class with all kinds of new information to share with their group!

So, after one class, what have students missed by not being placed in a traditional ensemble setting? They missed an opportunity to look at printed music. They have missed out learning how many beats a quarter note gets. They also missed a detailed explanation of correct guitar technique and posture, and they probably don't know the names of all the parts of the instrument. Hopefully, they also missed hearing "One, two, ready, play!" Please don't think I'm suggesting any of these things are not worthy of learning. That's not the point. The point is what they did learn. They learned to use their ear to listen within a small group of players. They learned how to cooperate in a learning setting with peers. They learned while teaching peers and being taught by peers. They began to get a sense of performing rhythmically by ear, and communicating with each other as they play. They learned in a very similar way to how people within our culture learn to play guitar. I am suggesting that these concerns are more important than the things that were skipped during this first class. Students concentrated on learning musical aspects instead of non-musical facets about the guitar.

It is not my intent, nor within the scope of this book, to provide specific teaching methods. Rather, the goal here is to contribute possibilities that might ignite your imagination. I'm certainly not suggesting a guitar class must begin with an E Major chord, or a specific strumming pattern, instead I am advocating for different approaches to teaching music. Approaches that students will find more relevant to their lives outside school. With the understanding that we are talking about just one potential approach for a class that could take many different shapes, let's continue. When students return for the second class (which could be the next day, or the next week, depending on the situation) you might immediately place them in their same groups and they can review what was covered the previous class. Each group can also work together on realizing the homework assignment and practicing transitioning between chords. You are playing the part of the mentor as you roam from group to group checking on progress, offering suggestions, checking for playing issues, observing group dynamics (which groups are working together and which are not), and getting a sense for who did the homework and who didn't. Notice that you are not the focus of the class, standing on a podium telling students what to do. Instead, the students are the focus of the class and they are taking on both traditional roles of teacher and student.

At some point you probably want to make some *brief* comments to the entire class concerning what you've observed and giving praise where it is deserved. You could also give students an opportunity to ask questions, but keep in mind that you want to get back to making music as quickly as possible. Since the students should have a functional ability with two chords you could now give them some creative freedom to use them within their groups. A song-writing assignment can take on many different shapes. Depending on the age and knowledge of the students, you could provide a good deal of structure or none at all. You might have them begin writing lyrics for a song or you could furnish lyrics (or perhaps just a topic). They would then need to add a strumming pattern to their chords and create a melody line for their lyrics. Be prepared: this could take a good deal of time! But this is time well spent. Think about what the students are doing ... they are being musicians in the best sense of the word. They are being composers, performers and listeners all at the same time! They are involved with self-directed, learner-centered, and peer-directed learning, and because they are making artistic decisions they will find a great sense of relevance with this work. One other thought about this type of assignment. Some groups will want to write things down. They might want to write out their lyrics. They may need to indicate which chord will be played at what time. They might even use some graphic notation to indicate other aspects of their song. But you don't need to be teaching how to notate anything! This assignment is about sound. It's not about the staff and quarter notes! The students will figure out ways to notate what they need.

What can you do with groups that finish their work before other groups? You don't want them sitting around idly, and you can only ask them to "play through your song again" so many times. You might suggest they try to add something to their song like another verse or a chorus. However, don't be surprised if they aren't interested in doing that. Often, when students tell you they are "finished," they don't mean only that their song is done, they mean they are "finished with it." You may have to accept that. If you composed a piece and played it for a friend, you probably don't want to hear them say it needs another section! There are, however, valid arguments regarding the advantages of having students revise and extend their creative work.[2]

It's quite likely there were song ideas generated by group members earlier in the process that were not used in the final song. You could ask the students to return to one of those ideas and do something with it. You could have them start working on additional chords and strumming patterns. Perhaps they might be interested in creating movement/dance for their song they might later teach to the class. Maybe you could make a video camera available for the group to record a performance of their piece in another room. Depending on the makeup of the group, you might temporally split them up and allow them to sit in with other groups that are still working. You may have to be creative, but you most likely don't want a group sitting around doing "nothing."

We should think a little about "noise" levels at this point. If you have twenty-something students all playing various things on guitars in one room ... it will be noisy. You might try to mediate the noise as you can, but there will be noise. I've been involved in situations like this innumerable times and students almost always find a way to make it work. I've even experienced positive results from such settings. I've had a student from one group who overheard something played by another group, and before I knew it groups are sharing and working on something together. Once in awhile you will probably need to ask a student or group to reduce their volume level, but typically this kind of setting will work. Of course, the larger the room, the better, and if you are really lucky you might have multiple areas to use as long as you are sure student well-being can be managed. You might also want to be prepared to explain to the principal what the students are doing if she happens to walk into your room when the noise level hits some peak! Make sure you frame your explanation in terms of student learning and musicianship.

Allowing adequate time for song-writing (or any creative work) is both necessary and challenging. The more you have students work creatively, the better you will get at judging how much time is right for your situation. Regardless, at some point you have to rein them all in and allow groups to share what they have been doing with the class. It's possible that some groups won't be "finished," but they still could share parts of what they have created. The groups shouldn't feel they need to perform a finished product. It's very likely you will get a good mix of results from the different groups, but keep in mind this is not a "formal" concert. Singing all the "right" notes with "correct" tone, and playing with "precise" rhythms, and being "perfectly" in tune aren't nearly as important in this setting as gaining meaning from the artistic experiences in which the students are involved. Be careful not to impose strict concepts of quality from formal concerts and other musical styles on these type of performances.

In-class performance time is a great opportunity for teaching as well. With each group performance you can make brief comments and suggestions. You could request student comments as well, or ask the class questions regarding each group's work and/or involve students in peer-assessment. No matter what, you want to make this a positive experience for all the groups and for each student. This is just the beginning of what should be many creative opportunities, and early successes will play an important role as the course continues.

So far we have students learning chords and song-writing, in a controlled size class, involved in a good deal of small group, learner-centered and peer-directed learning, making musical and creative decisions, performing in informal settings on instruments that are culturally relevant for them, not being burdened by traditional notation, all within a class setting in which students from any grade could enter and develop lifelong relevant musical skills. Not a bad start. This type of process could continue as students learn additional chords and strumming patters as well as more about guitar playing in general.

What about reproducing an existing song? Most certainly, students are going to want to cover popular songs they know. Most student groups become very motivated learning songs they like. Ask your groups of students to decide on a favorite song they would like to play on their guitars. The goal here is for them to pick a song that would get them excited. It's quite possible some students might want to change groups if another group is doing a song they like better. Allowing some fluidity might help the overall wellbeing of the class. Once songs are selected, the groups begin with listening to a recording of their song, and working on creating their version of it. You might allow students to locate and use web-based materials to help them (chord charts, for example).

Again, depending on the age of the students, and the level of their prior musical understanding, the process of copying a song by ear can take time. The amount of help students will need will vary wildly between groups. Consider what they are faced with. They have to try and match sounds from a recording to sounds they make on a guitar. Keep in mind that students in our class being described here may only know a handful of chords so far. Their work will require a lot of trial and error. Many will need your help naming and playing chords. Then they need to figure out how to play those chords. There are several ways you can help students learn new chords. You could supply printed charts for students to use. You could demonstrate chords for the students. You could make the internet available for them. And you need to always be aware of opportunities for students to teach each other – even across groups. This type of project could take several class meetings, so there would be plenty of opportunities for homework as well.

Some groups will have more success than others. Some groups will struggle because they picked a really hard song. This is actually a very good learning opportunity for students. It isn't unusual for a group of students to decide to change songs and this might allow you an opportunity to provide them with some suggestions. Almost certainly, the initial excitement with which students begin this type of project will fade to frustration. Your job, as teacher, is to keep the groups focused, and supply help as they need it. More often than not, they will slowly start to make breakthroughs, and in due time the excitement level will begin to build again. If you want to make the project "easier" you could select songs for the students to copy – songs that you know won't be as challenging. This might actually be a good plan for younger students, saving the opportunity for them to choose songs for succeeding copying projects. Overall, however, most students will work harder on songs they pick, regardless of difficulty. Why do students pick a particular song anyway? It's because they like the song, and that it has meaning to them. That is a pretty powerful combination. Students will learn quite a lot as they struggle. The next time they pick a song to copy they might start to look at other criteria as well. Just as before, this assignment requires you to make decisions about time. How much time will you give students before it's time for groups to perform their songs for the class? There is no easy answer, but the more you are involved with these types of learning situations, the better you will get at making such decisions. Keep in mind that it is not necessary for groups to have a song "finished" before they perform it for the class. Even performing fragments of songs can provide encouragement for students.

Well, there we go. I think we managed to get aspects of all the opportunities listed in Chapter 4 into this class:

- Small class size;
- Students allowed autonomy;
- Students making creative decisions;
- Emphasis on informal performances;
- Instruments and musical styles of interest to students;
- No real need for traditional notation;
- Students at any grade level could take part;
- Skills being learned that are relevant to the way students do music outside the schools, which is very likely to lead to lifelong interests for many students;

- And by the end of one year, or even a half-year, most students should be able to develop a functional command of the guitar (they would be able to continue making music in functional ways without you).

I haven't mentioned this yet, but I hope you also noticed that students in this guitar class are probably singing and playing an instrument. After all, songs have words, so there has to be playing and singing. This is another issue within many traditional school music programs. Especially at the secondary school level we have successfully divided music into two camps. There are choirs that sing and there are bands and orchestras that play instruments. It is rare to see significant examples where the two happen together. I've seen students in band classes who purposely belittle students in choir classes at the same school – and vice versa. Yet the vast majority of music in youth culture involves both singing and playing instruments side-by-side. We can do it in schools as well. We should be doing it in schools as well.

We need to address the idea of formal concerts a little. The primary performance outlet for our guitar class so far has been in-class performances. There will be a time when students will begin to want more. They'll want to show off the excitement they have with the guitar and the music they can make. The first reaction for many teachers would be to schedule a concert. While that is fine, I almost guarantee student attitudes in class would change. The learning environment would change. The goal becomes a concert. There would be less attention to making music, and more regard for getting ready for the concert. This isn't a bad thing on its own, however, we have all experienced how formal concert preparation can end up controlling the entire learning environment. Perhaps there are some alternatives that can get students out of the classroom, but in a less formal way. Let's start with the internet. The internet has created new definitions for many aspects of life, and continues to do so. The whole concept of what a "concert" can be has changed. The internet provides untold opportunities for student performances. What about a class website with a page devoted to each musical group? This could even become an aspect of the class, where students design their webpage to promote their music. Even appearances on the general school website would be a nice way to let the world know what students are doing in class. There are several great video-sharing websites as well. Some of these are very good in cases where student security is a concern. What about a podcast site? Students would be excited to share their music on a regularly updated podcast. What other online possibilities can you think of?

There are generally several in-school performance opportunities as well. Most schools have some sort of morning announcements where short performances could be featured. Perhaps the school has an outdoor courtyard area which might host an informal setting during certain parts of a school day. Entertainment in the lunchroom might be welcomed. Ask your students if there are areas in your school where they would like to perform. How about music before (and during) an evening event at the school, like a parent/teacher meeting, or a science fair? All of these can be presented with a different feel from a formal concert. Get your students off the stage and among the audience. Allow for interaction during performances with audience members. You need to go sit down and let the students be in charge. Work with teachers in your school that deal with other art forms. If your school has some sort of dance team, they might be excited to perform with live music. Perhaps there are students and/or teachers interested in theater or musicals (I was going to say drama, but we want to avoid that!). Wouldn't it be interesting to have students write their own musical that included original music, acting, dancing, staging, etc.? Again, the possibilities are limitless, often only restricted by our own imaginations (and sometimes funding!). By the way, you will discover a most amazing student attitude. When students are in charge of the creative aspects, they won't limit themselves to their present technical understanding. Instead, they will willingly extend themselves into previously unknown territory, and they will willingly work to develop the skills and technique they need. You will not have to ask them to practice, beg them to practice, require them to practice ... Instead, they will want to practice (Green, 2008).

Pause for Reflection

Most middle school and high school students in traditional ensembles do not practice as much as their teachers would like. This seems to be true in many colleges with music majors as well. Why do you think this is? What would be the advantages and disadvantages of the method suggested here?

We need to think about equipment. Just like a concert band, orchestra, or chorus, a guitar class will require instruments and some equipment. Let's start on the low end. If you plan to have classes of 20 students in guitar courses you will need at least 21 guitars (one for the teacher). There are a ton of choices and unless you know the possibilities well, you should sit down with an expert before ordering anything. Along with a modest supply of pics, extra strings, and some straps that could be enough to get a class started. You don't really need music stands or much sheet music since most activities can be sound (aural) based. If I could add one thing it would probably be cases for the guitars to help keep them from being damaged. Another add-on would be a small sound system with at least a couple microphones so vocalists can be heard, and to amplify guitar soloists or all the guitars. This can be very low end, or with enough funding can be more elaborate, including individual pickups and a larger mixing board. If you don't already know about them, you certainly want to investigate the Little Kids Rock organization (www.littlekidsrock.org) that helps teachers and schools with instruments and curriculum.

While the overall cost can be much higher, there are a couple of advantages to using electric guitars. The most important being that the guitar itself doesn't make sound. The expense comes from having to add equipment for sound reinforcement, but if funding is possible, a very classroom-friendly setup can be achieved. You would first need the 20 student electric guitars. In groups of four or five, run these into a mixer (you would need four mixers if you used groups of five, or five mixers with groups of four … I'm pretty good with math!). The mixer would then connect to a separate headphone mixer, and each student would wear a pair of headphones allowing them to hear the entire group. Now you have four or five separate groups of students, in one room, all playing different things at the same time, and all they can hear is their own group! Plus, when the principal drops by, the room is as quiet as can be! To make this setup really effective you could add microphones for students to talk and sing into. This would require larger mixers, but it adds yet more functionality. With this type of setup you would only need one sound system for the room that students could plug into to present work to the class. You might be surprised that an entire system like this, including 20 electric guitars and microphones, five mixers, five headphone mixers, 20 headphones, sound system for the room, plus all the necessary cables and wires, could be purchased for less than the cost of one Selmer Model 41 Contra Bass Clarinet![3]

Speaking of instruments, we are now just one step away from turning our guitar class into a "band" class. If we add some electric bass guitars, some keyboards, and electric drums we have five bands instead of five guitar groups. Using the headphone mixers, we still have a pretty quiet classroom and a lot of music making would be going on! Additionally (or alternately), the same type setup could include DJ controllers, mixing decks, and/or digital music instruments (check out the Maschine Jam and Ableton Push). Then there is (at least) one more step we could take to make this class really remarkable. With the addition of a computer for each group we could add recording, mixing, and producing to the class. Now students can compose, listen, perform, and be recording engineers. I can't imagine a K-12 school in the country where such a class (in any of its variations) wouldn't be immensely popular and meaningful for students.

Tablet-Based Performance Class

In Chapter 4, I purposely choose to compare an oboe, as a traditional musical instrument, to an iPad, as a non-traditional musical instrument. The iPad (as well as similar app-based devices) brings a whole new world of possibilities to music performance. The touch interface is a big part of this, but even more important is the ever-growing library of musical apps that are available – and most can be purchased at very low cost! The variety of musical apps is truly amazing, and the array of different sound possibilities is staggering. Never have so many sound choices been so easily accessible. Almost anything is possible when multiple iPads (or other portable devices) are played together. You have access to almost any traditional instrument sound. There are apps that make clarinet, trumpet, and violin sounds (more on this in a minute). There are apps for almost every percussion instrument on the face of the earth. There are apps for instruments of the world you have never heard of, and there are apps that make sounds no other instrument in the world can make. And finally, if there are sounds you want to make for which you can't find apps – there are apps that allow you to record, edit, and manipulate any sound for use in playback. There are several music performance apps, and more appear all the time. You might even create a new music app yourself! The possibilities are truly endless!

With so many different apps and sounds, what are we likely to hear coming from a music room during an iPad class? We might hear some hip-hop. We might hear some country and western, or metal, or rap, or African drumming, or steel drums, or electronic dance music, or classic rock, or Monteverdi, or the Beatles, or aleatoric music, or a pipe organ, or a string ensemble, or a theremin, or a DJ battle, or a percussion ensemble, or unusual electronic bleeps and blasts and beeps, or a folk song with guitar accompaniment, or a gamelan ensemble, or a piano solo. Do you get the idea? And this list is only the beginning!

I mentioned there are apps that make clarinet, trumpet and violin sounds, and there is a good chance this made you grimace. It is important for performers of acoustic instruments to give some thought about "synthesized" or "sampled" sounds. More and more, acoustic instruments are being replaced by instruments that produce synthesized and sampled sounds. If you play a traditional acoustic instrument you have probably spent thousands of hours working to get just the right sound. You've most likely had teachers stress the importance of obtaining the proper characteristic sounds of your instrument. That particular sound is very important to you. For many performers of traditional acoustic instruments (maybe you as well?) it really doesn't matter how good the technology gets, they are never likely to be satisfied with synthesized representations. For many traditional performers, synthesized and sampled sounds just aren't "good enough." However, there is a stark reality that is very important to understand. There are very few other people who care. Libby Larson suggests we have arrived at a time when most people actually *prefer* synthesized sound over acoustic sound.[4] Music in our culture has been dominated by this sound (which Larson refers to as "produced sound") since before most of today's K-12 students were even born. In all likelihood, these sounds are just as important to them as acoustic sound probably is to you. It simply doesn't matter to students what instruments produced the lush sounding string instrument sound in a favorite song. You might raise your eyebrow and be put out that "real" violin players weren't used to make the recording, but most people *simply don't care*. What you might want to believe is a very big deal is a non-issue for most people in our society – especially school-aged students. Remember what I told you in Chapter 1? More than anything else, this book is about change. Musical sound isn't "changing," it has changed. You don't have to like the change, but you have to respect it. Those who continue to hold on to the past after change has occurred are often seen as irrelevant. This is where we are quickly headed in the schools as we continue to ignore changes in our society and in musical culture. I was recently at a conference and heard a presenter talk about change in the medical profession. He said that doctors who learned their craft 20 years ago and persist practicing what they know are continually moving closer to malpractice. Think about that …

What is the experience making music on an iPad like? In many ways it is a very similar experience to making music on any other musical instrument (even the oboe!). You learn certain techniques and skills required for each app, you practice, and (ideally) you develop musicality as you progress with the instrument. Some apps are pretty simple and playing technique can be learned quickly. Other apps, however, are quite complex and require substantial practice in order to perform well. The sheer number of musical apps serves to increase the complexity of performing on the instrument as the necessary set of techniques are so diverse. One of the most important differences, however, between making music on an iPad and making music on most traditional instruments concerns immediacy. Many apps allow for almost immediate musical sounds. While practice will almost always improve outcomes, you can make truly musical sounds on many apps from the first touch. This is seldom true on traditional instruments. Such immediacy is often viewed by traditional performers as "cheating." Obviously, this view would suggest, making musical sounds with so little effort is not as honorable, and it somehow lessens the musical experience. This attitude could be considered "sour grapes." Perhaps "envy" is a nicer way to put it. After all, "since I put in so much work turning squeaks and squawks into music on the clarinet, everyone should have to do it this way." What this attitude misses is how much quicker students might progress in the development of real musicianship when, from the very start, the sounds they make are musical in nature. Something similar must have occurred during the early 1800s when valves were added to trumpets. Players of the natural trumpet most certainly resented those who first began learning on valved instruments. Playing with valves would obviously have been considered cheating. How could anything so easy be considered good? Come to think of it, it's surprising the whole valve thing actually caught on (sarcasm is dripping from those words). Let me say it again, those who continue to hold on to the past after change has occurred are often seen as irrelevant. There isn't much need for players of the natural trumpet these days.

What might an iPad music class look like? While there are certainly many possibilities, it could very closely follow the model of the guitar class. To start with, an iPad music class should probably be limited to the average class size as other academic classes in a particular school. While this seems like a pretty simple matter, it represents a major shift in thinking for many music educators. Bigger isn't always better. If 120 students want to take a particular class, that would be a full-time teaching load at most schools – not one class! Our iPad music class could use the same learner-centered, peer-directed groupings of students where three to five students work cooperatively making creative decisions concerning composing, arranging, and performance. Student groups would be placed around the room, or in other spaces as are available. Students would also make choices concerning which instrument sounds to use and what musical styles to involve. The music teacher would serve several roles while helping students develop independent musicality. They would furnish assignments, provide direct instruction as needed, and serve as a mentor, coach, and encourager. Early assignments (depending on student ages) might simply help students explore some of the many sound possibilities of the instrument. These could lead to creative assignments within certain parameters. As with the guitar class, students could have opportunities to aurally copy songs that interest them. As soon as is feasible, students should also be allowed to have input on assignments. The teacher's role then is to make sure students continue to develop musically as they realize their own direction in the class. The teacher's role will probably be more active with younger, less musically experienced students, but in all cases the teacher would ideally become less and less of a force in the class as the weeks go by.

The main goal of the class would be independent musicianship instead of formal concerts, but there would certainly be opportunities for students to show off their work. Traditional notation would be involved in cases where it was necessary to achieve the needs of the students. For example, if students wanted to play a portion of a classical piece from a notated source using traditional string instrument sounds, they would need to develop sufficient reading skills. They will probably have a high level of intrinsic motivation to learn to read notation in a situation like this, and the results are quite likely to be much better than if you forced it on them (Deci and Ryan, 2002). However, an important goal of the class should not be for students to learn to read and write traditional music notation as it is quite probable the greater majority of their work in the class would not require these skills. There would be no need for any specific prior musical involvement in order to join such a class, making it available to students in any grade level. A course like this could be repeated by students more than once. Beginner students might be placed in groups with more experienced students. This arrangement could be beneficial to both the beginning and experienced students as they work in a cooperative environment. While the option to repeat the course could be available, those students who choose not to, or are unable to take the course more than once, are still quite likely to develop meaningful lifelong musical skills because of the class setup.

An iPad class would have very similar equipment needs, and possibilities, as with the guitar class. On the low end each student would need an iPad and probably a small portable speaker. That would be enough to get going. All the options available for the guitar class would also be possible for the iPad class. A group of iPads could be connected to a mixer. The mixer could be connected to either a set of speakers, or a headphone mixer. When using the amplifier, each student would then wear a set of headphones which would allow them to hear all the iPads from the group. Again, the addition of microphones would allow for talking, singing, humming, rapping, beatboxing, and so on. Except for exchanging iPads for guitars, this setup can be almost identical to the guitar class setup, and the overall cost would be fairly similar – very close to the cost of one Fox Model 101 Bassoon!

So, we have two classes that are quite similar both in setup and function. One would use guitars (or added bass, drums, and keyboards to make bands), the other iPads (or other portable digital devices). Of course, there is nothing keeping you from combining the two and creating a "music class." What about that? A music performance, composition, song-writing, improvisation, and production class that makes use of guitars, bass guitars, keyboards, iPads, microphones, and drums. Students are making musical decisions, singing, rapping, and playing music they enjoy and/or create themselves, all on instruments they prefer, in a meaningful and culturally relevant setting that is quite likely to provide them with lifelong musicianship skills. Many students would find the possibilities exhilarating!

You could also discover something interesting, and perhaps unexpected, in a music-making class like this. You might find a student in the class who has experience playing the cello and they want to add this to a song their group is working on. Maybe a student wants to learn to play the cello (or accordion, or trombone, or bag-pipes, etc.) for a certain song. If you, or they, have access to the instrument, give them some guidance and let the student learn and make music. You might even be approached by a student that's not in the class who wants to join it so they can make music on a zither they found at home in a closet. How cool would that be?

Pause for Reflection

Traditionally we have devised music classes so that a student focuses on one instrument the entire time they participate. The idea presented here would allow students to change from instrument to instrument as they feel they need to. What do you think of that concept? What would be some advantages to this method?

Music Technology Class

The first two settings we've looked at are live performance-based, so let's move now to some possibilities that are less about performance, but cover other important aspects of music. The business of music has undergone amazing changes in the past couple of decades. Trades that were once only available for a few select individuals, and that required massive amounts of funding, are now open to almost anyone. There are several new opportunities for school music course offerings involving electronic and digital technologies that many students would find interesting, but first the profession has to move beyond pessimistic thinking concerning music technology. There are at least four issues that very often get in the way of offering music technology courses in schools. 1) *Music made with computers is "sterile" and not of sufficient quality.* This thinking is simply an extension of the stance that raises Western European classical music in status above all other musical styles. If one of our goals is to alienate as many students as possible, then this line of thinking should do the trick. You know not to compare apples to oranges, but do you know why? What makes an apple good would make a pretty nasty orange. I prefer firm, crunchy apples – a firm crunchy orange not so much. There are good apples and bad apples, good oranges and bad oranges. Apples and oranges are both fruits but you can't compare them to each other.

The same is true of music. What makes a classical symphony good would make a pretty nasty rock song, Indian raga, or dubstep piece. There are good classical symphonies and bad classical symphonies, good rock songs and bad rock songs. Classical symphonies and rock songs are both musics but you can't compare them to each other. Music created with electronic and digital instruments can be done well or poorly. It can be musical or non-musical. It can be full of life or sterile. The same is true of music created with a symphony orchestra. It's the same with every style of music – it isn't about the instruments, it's about the people making the music. Students can be taught the difference and they can learn to make better music in any style. It's time to get past the belief that the music "I" take pleasure in is better than the music "you" enjoy. Outdated, arrogant views about the quality of music you might not personally appreciate are absolutely unacceptable, as well as detrimental for the future of music education.

2) *Students already know about technology.* Actually, the opposite is more often the case. Even at the college level I'm amazed by the number of students that have no real music technology skills. These are students (this was you perhaps?) that have grown up with easily assessible music technology all around them, but for whatever reasons they haven't taken advantage of it. Certainly there will be a handful of students in given K-12 schools that have become proficient with music technology (more on these students in a minute). There will be several that dabble, but you can bet there are *many* that would love the opportunity to learn about making music with electronic and digital technologies. This is actually the underlying notion for this entire chapter. I am confident that the majority of students at any given school in the country would relish an opportunity at their school to become more musical in ways that are meaningful and relevant to them. That should be the role of the *music teachers* in a school – to meet these students where they are musically and bring them forward in ways that are meaningful and relevant to them!

3) *I don't know enough about music technology to teach it.* Please pardon my bluntness for a moment – do something about it! If your goal is to teach music, then you should consider it an obligation to know as much as you can about the various methods of music making that our culture makes available. I think a school music teacher should be embarrassed acting as the school's "musical expert" if in fact he is really only knowledgable about one particular musical genre. If you feel you can't get started on your own then take a class. Get together with other students and ask for help from faculty that could help you. Use the internet for assistance. The only method that is sure not to work is sitting around waiting for the knowledge and skills to somehow just happen. Don't for a second believe that music making with electronic

and digital instruments is going to go away and that your future students will not be interested in it!

Let's return to the students I mentioned a bit ago; those that are already proficient with music technology – and even those that "dabble." Many of these students would also be excited to take a music technology class in school and I'm sure some would enroll. So now we have an issue ... you could be the teacher in a class where some of the students know much more about the technology used in the class than you do. What do you think of that? I'd suggest it's not much different than being a high school band director. I'll use myself as an example. I was a clarinet player. Over the years I was fortunate to have several students who were All-State quality performers on instruments other than clarinet. They had more performance knowledge of their instruments (technology) than did I. What I had was a more expanded and wider sense of musicianship and creativity and I could add to their musical understanding even though they had more technique on their instrument. The same would be true in almost any music technology setting. I would certainly have students who could teach me about how the equipment worked, but I would be able to help guide them with making music. It can be a truly wonderful combination of teaching and learning where everyone wins.

4) And finally, *Technology is too expensive*. This can be true depending on how you look at it. If you see purchases to support a music technology class as an add-on only after every band/choir/orchestra need is take care of, then yes, technology may be too expensive. If the needs of a technology class are seen to be as important as those for traditional offerings, then you might be surprised. The cost of many pieces of technology equipment is less than some traditional instruments. Keep in mind you don't have to start off with the "best" equipment, or the industry-standard software, or full classroom sets of hardware. You can start small and grow. Oftentimes schools will already have some equipment that you could borrow or use for music purposes, and sometimes there is available funding for "technology" that can't be used for other purchases. I will have a few other funding ideas below, but I believe it comes down to attitude. When you feel something is important enough (like the development of a child's musical understanding) you will find ways to make it happen.

The reality is, "music made with computers is not as good; students already know about technology; I don't know enough; and, the cost is too high," are excuses. Often we use excuses to cover up the real issues. I'm afraid all too often the real issue keeping music teachers from embracing music technology is that they don't want to. This is a serious issue. I hope those that feel this way might take a look in the mirror and really consider why it is they want to teach music. Do you seriously want to reach all students with musical possibilities, or are you only interested in the few students that think like you did when you were in middle and high school?

The great thing about music technology is *the rate of advancement with which it moves and changes*. It can be a very exciting field! However, the problem with music technology is *the rate of advancement with which it moves and changes*. It can be a very difficult field in which to remain current! There are a lot of students that would take on this excitement and challenge with eagerness. With the understanding that things in technology can change quickly, and realizing there can be a tremendous amount of overlap between the different examples, let's overview a couple of the many course options that would fit into this category.

Music Production Class

Music production could mean several things, but here I'm specifically thinking of a production setting where students are using digital hardware and software to create music. Such a course might also be called a digital composition class or a song-writing class. Students would use computers and/or tablets, and various midi and digital input devices, to compose and arrange music through specific software. Traditionally, this software has been known as sequencing software, but it could just as well be considered production software. A more current term for this type of setup is "digital audio workstation" or DAW.

Students in such a class would arrange existing sound files, and/or sound files they create, to produce new music. Talk about endless possibilities! Through the use of sequencing, sampling, and recording, an entire world of sound is available. Students who enjoy music and working with digital music devices would flock to a course like this. And in case you were not aware, there are a lot of students who enjoy music and working with digital music devices.

Most production software allows the user to arrange sounds in various sequences and in several layers to produce new music. In addition to using previously created sound files, students can record and/or create their own sounds using any sound source they choose. They can then manipulate these sounds in several different ways, and layer them in an assortment of tracks so that different sounds can overlap. This type of class could be project-based, and the teacher's role would be to assign projects for students and then to provide both technical and musical assistance as necessary. Students, in this setting, would probably work independently most of the time, to produce music that completes assignments. Creating original music is often a very personal process and students may find it difficult doing group work in such a class. It is feasible, however, for pairs of students to cooperate on various projects. This might be true for an initial project for very young students, for example.

An important question for teachers in a hardware-/software-based class involves students learning how to use the technology. There are at least a couple of approaches to this. One way would be to teach the technology first, making sure students understand how to function within the particular software. Another way, and probably more preferable, would be to provide a series of short projects that students would complete as they learn the capabilities of the software. This is especially good if the results of these introductory projects could then be reused in more advanced projects later. The goal would be to get to music making as quickly as possible. It's the same issue in beginner band classes. Students want to make music and they are bored too often, taking the preliminary steps necessary to get them there. Anything you can do that would allow students to make music quickly is worth the effort. A music technology class needs to be more about the music than the technology.

Just as there is an unlimited number of sound possibilities for students to use, there is a wide variety of project types from which to choose. Students could be asked to produce a 30-second commercial, with music and speaking (and/or singing) to advertise a product. They could compose pieces in the style of certain genres of music, perhaps with some twists thrown in for fun. They could write their own rap, or compose music to accompany a story or dramatic reading. Consider the possibilities of working with language arts teachers in your school with this! Another great way to connect with your school is to ask fellow teachers if they have a need for some music to use with their classes, and put your students to the tasks. Students might score a video or film. They could create a piece that combines recorded sounds and live performance where their produced piece plays along with live performers. The possibilities, again, are only limited by our imaginations. And when your imagination runs dry, make sure you allow students to design projects as well – in fact, make sure you do this before you are out of ideas!

Pause for Reflection

When you allow students to create music they like, it's quite possible they will often times generate music that you "don't like." How might you handle that? What are the ramifications of this?

Recording Arts Class

The world of music recording is a very different place than it used to be. Digital technologies have changed the entire look and feel of this field. Unlike the days when it took hundreds of thousands of dollars to even begin, today a person can practice as a recording artist from their home for a small fraction of that cost, and still have the potential of producing studio quality work. Providing students in schools opportunities to develop skills in the field of recording arts could be very popular at any level of education.

A course in recording arts could focus on any of a variety of different concepts and techniques. While there would certainly be some overlap between different courses, there isn't any one particular model that would necessarily be better than another. A lot would depend on the age of students involved, the amount of class time available, and the type of equipment at the teacher's disposal. Following are five potential dimensions that might be addressed in a typical recording arts class:

1) Sound Fundamentals. Understanding concepts of sound is an important aspect of recording. This would include concepts like amplitude, sound waves, and basic acoustics; critical listening skills regarding intonation, pitch, balance, and tone; the ability to troubleshoot audio hardware and software; and understanding microphone, technique, use, and placement.

2) Music Production. Students should have some understanding of the fundamental principles of how sound is produced on a variety of instruments and voice. Skills in basic song-writing would also be very important.

3) Recording. Hands-on work with audio recording equipment would be essential. This would include learning how to run a live recording session, including mixing and editing techniques for music and dialogue.

4) Postproduction. Students could develop skills creating and recording sound effects, editing dialogue, overlaying sounds, and creating final projects for music, video, radio, television, and video games. In cases where the necessary equipment was available, editing techniques for surround-sound would also be important.

5) Marketing. A final area that would be helpful for students interested in sound recording would be an understanding of the music business, including knowledge of how to market, distribute, and manage.

There are obvious financial issues with a recording arts type course as the hardware and software requirements could be prohibitively expensive. Gaining access to already existing school labs and equipment might be a good place to start. Many schools have audio equipment which music teachers might be able to use. Another strategy could include cooperative projects with other teachers. Principals might be willing to purchase new equipment if several areas within a school could make use of it in cooperative ways. Further possibilities might involve applying for technology grants, or contacting local organizations that are replacing existing equipment with new purchases. Often companies are willing to donate used hardware to schools or sell it at a significant savings. Despite the challenges, a recording arts course could be a popular addition in most schools as many students would be interested in the technology and also recognize the marketability of the skills they would be eager to learn. As a possible extension to a recording arts course, a music teacher could team with other teachers in a school to offer one or more opportunities combining various media including music, dance, film, and video. Students developing recording skills would also be able to assist with live performances and broadcasts. Such a mixed media course would have several significant advantages for students as they would gain experience with a variety of musical settings, all with real-world music business implications.

Regardless of the specific course content, the design of a recording arts course could be very similar to the other class settings at which we've looked. You would want to control class size as with any other academic course. Students would work as individuals and in small cooperative groups. They should be allowed as much control over their learning as is possible, including the authority to make musical and creative decisions within musical styles of their choosing, and input regarding the overall direction of the course. There would be significant opportunities for student work to be presented in and outside of class, and not only in formal "concerts." Students would work with whatever instruments are available to them and in combinations of their choosing, which could certainly include traditional wind and string instruments. There would be little to no need for training in traditional music notation, but aspects of notation could be included in specific cases as necessary. Students would certainly find relevance in such a course and it would be quite possible for them to develop a functional skill level within one year or less. And finally, while there would be potential for multiple levels of the course (Recording Arts I, Recording Arts II, Recording Arts III, etc.), beginning and advanced students could easily be mixed in one section, and students could comfortably begin at any grade level.

I know you are aware of how pervasive electronic and digital music is in our present musical culture. There is no indication that it will slow down anytime soon – in fact, the digital "revolution" continues to expand. It is a perfect time for the music education profession to fully embrace these types of musical understandings to help students develop musicality they will be able to make use of their rest of their lives. This will bring us to a fourth setting, also having to do with technology, but in a very different way. However, one more thought first.

As we've discussed previously (yes, I'm bringing it up again), our profession is devoted to the idea that being musical must include the ability to read and write standard music notation. If you felt this way before, I hope you are at least reconsidering it. I keep coming back to this because it's that important. Yes, it is absolutely necessary for students to read notation in order to get the most out of our traditional ensembles, but this is simply not true for most other musical styles. This holds especially true for most music technology settings. However, our devotion to notation also extends to technology. Too often, music teachers see music notation programs as a necessary technology for students. I suggest the place for music notation software should be music classes in which performance practice requires reading and writing skills. It would be quite helpful, in fact, if music teachers had band, choir, and orchestra students involved with music notation software, especially at beginning levels (even though I seldom see this in practice). However, very few fields of music technology or music business have any significant need for these skills. Just as it is important to get past the belief that music notation skills are necessary for all types of music settings, we need to move beyond the idea that *music technology begins with music notation* programs. The time to help a student (or students) build notational literacy is when they decide for themselves that they want to learn about it. Their motivation at that point will produce amazing results.

Internet-Based Music Class

The way many music teachers (and other classically trained musicians, for that matter) behave, you would think the internet is a passing fad. Most music teachers see little to no academic use for the internet, preferring to use it primarily for communication through a variety of means (email, webpages, social networking, etc.). If you were to take a look at the music site from different schools' web pages you would most likely see the dissemination of information for students and parents, and stories and pictures of events (most notability, performances). Some teachers will post assignments and/or due dates, and perhaps some tutorials, but there simply isn't much music teaching going on at the K-12 levels that makes use of the internet.

Virtual schooling has proliferated during the past two decades. Entire college degree programs are available online. Many states have K-12 virtual schools where students can complete much of their required and elective coursework without setting foot on a "campus." The legislature in Florida recently decided that *all* high school students must complete at least one online class as a graduation requirement. Online learning is still only in its infancy, but it is already a very big deal and it will not go away. Yet online music offerings, outside of music appreciation type courses and AP music theory, are still relatively few. Why is this? I'd suggest a lot of it comes down to what we know ... we know traditional ensembles. Unfortunately, running a traditional band, choir, or orchestra rehearsal over the internet still isn't practical. Given time, the technology may certainly get there, but we aren't there yet. So, the response from music teachers about teaching a music class online is usually – it can't be done. Just as it tends to be with face-to-face options, the profession is blind to many possibilities.

This is a good time to give some thought to the internet. In a very short period of time it has changed the way people do things. It has literately changed how we live. The changes keep coming every day, and the rate of change is growing faster all the time. We can't even imagine what the internet will be like ten years from now, but one thing is certain – the internet is changing the look and feel of how people learn. It is changing what is meant by "school." Our profession wants to believe the internet will not affect what we do – that it will be ok to continue in our little world of music making just like we have always done and ignore internet wrought change. But that would be a serious mistake. Assuming you are on a path to beginning a career in music education, you need to keep in mind that you are the future of our profession. It is quite possible you could still be teaching in 20 or even 30 years. If you haven't begun considering how the internet will affect your future as a music teacher over that span of time, you should start now. Not doing so could be a very serious mistake. I would go so far as to suggest it is very likely that you will be asked to teach music online at some point in your teaching career.

So if doing large ensemble rehearsals over the internet isn't practical today, what is? The answer, I'm afraid, is whatever you set your mind to do. Let me suggest that the ten opportunities set forth in Chapter 4 make a very good place to begin. Since you can't stand over your students to control their every move, the internet is actually the perfect place for coursework that is learner-centered and self-directed. It provides an optimum setting where students are free to make creative decisions, choose instruments and musical styles of their liking, and develop functional musicality. In many ways, the internet provides an ideal learning environment in which students can establish lifelong skills.

Online courses can be either taught synchronously or asynchronously. The former requires students and teachers to be present online at the same time. The latter allows students to do work on their own time, often within certain constraints, but without the requirement of being online at specific times. There is a considerable difference, however, between an asynchronous online class and a correspondence course model where students would work at their own pace. Normally, asynchronous courses will have specific deadlines for individual assignments so that all students in a course are working on the same material during the same period of time so that interactions between students will be more meaningful. A course using a combination of synchronous and asynchronous learning would require some specific online encounters, but allow students to work on their own beyond those times.

The content of online music classes can be very similar, if not identical, to the same course offered face-to-face. The teacher should have the same high expectations for students' work, and can require students to be just as punctual turning in assignments. Additionally, there are two characteristics of successful online courses that play important roles in helping students learn. Both are related to communication. First is the ability to interact. Without the face-to-face contact of traditional education, it is imperative that students be provided the ability to easily collaborate with each other. Second is the availability of the teacher. The teacher of an online course needs to make themselves readily available for student questions and must be willing to provide significant feedback for all course work. An online course cannot be expected to succeed if students are unable to work collaboratively or if the teacher is not highly involved in the course. Finally, any school interested in successful online course experiences must make adequate technical support available. The teacher's role should be that of content specialist. The technology has not advanced yet to the point where the teacher should be expected to both teach and be the technical expert. More and more schools, and school systems, are investing in the types of technical assistance music teachers would require to make online music courses succeed. What a great question that would make for you to ask at your first job interview!

Assuming we leave out large ensembles as online possibilities, what is left? Let's start with a music composition, song-writing, or music production-type course. These could actually work very well in an online environment. An important difference, of course, from offering this in a face-to-face situation is that students would now be responsible for supplying the necessary hardware and software. On first thought this might seem like a negative, but let's think about it for a minute. Funding for initial technology purchases in schools is seldom easy. Even when this is possible, updating and maintaining often become serious problems. It takes a continuing stream of funding to keep technology functioning and up-to-date in a school setting. Removing this burden from the budget might create opportunities in some schools where they did not otherwise exist. So the requirement for particular hardware and software becomes the responsibility of the student, and obviously this could keep some students from being able to participate. With this in mind, the teacher could reduce the hardware/software requirements of the course which might open the door to more students. For example, instead of requiring industry-standard software, a less powerful version could be used in the class, which might also allow students to use older, or less expensive hardware. Additionally, there is a growing number of free music software titles available online.

There are also obvious advantages to students owning their own equipment. We see this with traditional instrumental ensembles. Students who own their instrument are more often in a better situation than students who have to borrow or rent an instrument. Students who take an in-school technology-based course but do not have the hardware/software at home will not be able to complete certain assignments outside of class time. However, students with their own technology will be able to continue working with music applications at any time. Additionally, when a particular music course is completed, the student who has access to the technology at home will be more apt to continue working with it and developing more advanced skills. There is a lot to think about!

The content of an online music composition, song-writing, or music production-type course could be identical to a face-to-face class. Students would probably work on their own most of the time completing projects, but they could work in pairs on some assignments just as they would in the in-school class. As mentioned earlier, it would be very important for students to be able to interact online with each other, discussing their work, and sharing ideas, works in progress, and final projects. It is actually amazing how similar the two settings for such a course could be. All the assignments and activities comprising the live course could also be included online. One surprising aspect of online learning is the potential for interactivity. Students in an online course can actually spend more time working together than is customary in standard face-to-face classes. The reason for this is that online courses are not bound to start and end times. Class doesn't "start" at a certain time on a certain day. And it doesn't end really until the end of the semester or year. Online classes can involve students at any time, seven days a week. There are really no weekends or holidays for online classes as students could be participating in class activities at any time. I have found that I actually get to know my students better through online classes than in traditional settings because we tend to interact for a much greater amount of time.

If you want to be even more adventurous, there is another possibility. One class could be offered in both formats at the same time. Those students who could meet live would attend a face-to-face portion, and those students who couldn't meet live would be online. Imagine a class combining students that are physically in your school, with students from other parts of your school district, state, nation, or world! The online version could be synchronous, so that distance students would be required to "attend" at the same time through a video/audio connection, or it could be asynchronous so that online students view a recorded version of class meetings. This version could allow students in the same school to attend in cases when they have a schedule conflict that wouldn't allow them to take your class face-to-face. A blended course such as this can be tricky as it is important that online students receive the exact same opportunities as the face-to-face students. For example, it would be important for the teacher to offer online students the same amount of time to ask questions and to receive individual assistance with classwork. Beyond class time, however, students in both formats would interact together online just as if they were all "online" students. There really is a lot to think about!

Other online class possibilities might include a song-writing class, or perhaps a popular music history course with a song-writing element. Even the guitar class we looked at earlier in this chapter would be possible. Live performance over the internet, with multiple performers, can still be challenging, depending on the speed of the connections potential students have available. But it is certainly plausible for two students to play online together. In cases where connection speeds don't allow for "live" combined performance, one student could record their part, and another student could then record over the first – a performance-/recording-type class. Just imagine the possibilities – a student in Iowa writing music and playing along with a student in Japan! The possibilities are, again, only limited by our imaginations. Almost anything is possible when the teacher sees issues as opportunities. And very little is possible when they are seen as roadblocks. There is a whole new world of opportunities out there today. Opportunities to bring exciting, relevant music offerings to a wildly diverse group of students who are not interested in the traditional way in which we have practiced music in the schools. What possibilities can you imagine?

How might you learn more about teaching music classes online? First, check out tutorials that are available on video-sharing websites. You might just be amazed how much is available! Look at these with an eye to the teaching/learning environment. Sure you might learn something about the content, but the goal here is to think about what the teacher is doing and how students might interact with the material. If you haven't already, you might also take an online music class yourself. It doesn't have to be offered by your school (but that would be great as well). In fact, it could be *any* music class. You might investigate an area of music that you know little about. Finally, you should try to teach something yourself at-a-distance! Maybe you could include an online unit, or part of a unit, as a portion of your student teaching experience!

It's quite possible you may have only been thinking of these four settings (guitar classes, internet-based classes) with secondary schools in mind. However, aspects of all these would work quite well at the elementary school level. Elementary school general music needs to be perceived as something more than preparation for those students who might later participate in traditional performing ensembles. Elementary-aged students would enjoy working with guitars, iPads, and music technology including production software and recording hardware or mixed media, and they could also benefit from internet-based learning opportunities. Besides the "enjoyment" factor, students at the elementary school level would find these interactions just as relevant as older students, and they will be just as likely to develop functional levels of musicality through them. All the opportunities discussed in Chapter 4 would apply to elementary school music classes as well. In addition to teacher-led activities, students should be allowed opportunities for self-directed, learner-centered, and small peer-group learning. They must be given significant opportunities for making their own musical and creative decisions. They should be able to interact with instruments and musical styles that interest them. Notation reading experiences need to be directly tied to activities that make use of the notation, and not as separate lessons taught for the sake of doing it. The same type of informal performing we discussed in Chapter 4 would be just as applicable for elementary students. In fact, at this level it might be more beneficial to reduce the number of formal performances so that the precious little time elementary music teachers get with their students can be used to focus more on individual musicianship. It is just as important for younger learners to perceive relevance in what they do in school as it is for older students.

An Additional Possibility

One final idea that I hinted at before ... an amazing course in music might include any combination of instruments and musical styles that students in your school find meaningful. Students, collaboratively and creatively, working in small groups creating hip-hop, blues, country, pop, classical, rock, barbershop, EDM, salsa – using guitars, bass guitars, drum sets, keyboards, iPads, microphones, digital hardware/software, recording, mixing, production and video equipment, cellos, violins, clarinets, zithers, accordions, trombones, xylophones, bass drums, and cowbells ... and anything else to which you and/or students have access. Then throw in the ten opportunities from Chapter 4 in various combinations, letting students make decisions about what they want to accomplish, with you serving as a guide, mentor, and advisor, and you have the potential for a very exciting musical experience for your students and yourself. Don't hold back on any possibilities – allow acting, dancing, lighting, staging, and anything your students can imagine. I'm not sure what you would call this class – maybe "Make Your Music," or

"Music for All." What a cool basis for a music class – where any student could make music they want to make, in ways they want to make it, while being helped by a teacher. I would think it could become a very popular option at almost any school. Imagine the possibilities, imagine the potential learning that could occur, imagine the levels of musicianship students might reach, imagine the school principal thinking you were pretty awesome!

Pause for Reflection

What do you think of this final class possibility? What do you believe students would think of it? What would you need to do to prepare yourself to offer such a music class? What course names can you think of for this class?

In Chapter 2 I provided a historical snapshot of our profession because it is important for you to understand how and why music education in the United States got its start. Included was a look at what was going on musically in our society and how this influenced the way music was approached in schools. In Chapter 3 we overviewed changes that have occurred in our society since the time music entered the schools in the United States, including changes that have affected the way music is practiced within the society. It is vital that we acknowledge how these changes, along with our profession's resistance to change, have contributed to making music as practiced in the schools irrelevant to the vast majority of students. Then in Chapter 4, I suggested we have several opportunities to make music education more relevant for students in schools, however, these opportunities will require change. Finally, in this chapter we explored some possibilities for the implementation of these opportunities. These possibilities are not meant as a definitive listing of all our options, but instead, as a place where we might begin. At this point in our history there is a need for a sense of urgency. The future of music education in the schools is dependent on taking advantage of opportunities for change – and it needs to start now. As the future of music education, you have an opportunity to help return music in the schools to a place of real significance.

Notes

1 See Class Guitar Resources (www.classguitar.com) for example. They supply student textbooks, guitar ensemble books and teacher manuals.

2   Peter Webster and Jackie Wiggins are strong advocates for revision in student composition. For example see Webster's chapter, "What do you mean, make my music different? Encouraging revision and extensions in children's music composition," in: Maud Hickey's 2003 publication, *Why and How to Teach Music Composition: A New Horizon for Music Education,* published by NAfME, and Wiggins' 1990 *Composition in the Classroom: A Tool for Teaching* (also published by NAfME), and her 2009, 2nd edition of *Teaching for Musical Understanding,* published by the Center for Applied Research in Musical Understanding.

3   One representative setup could include:

> 20 Fender Standard Statocaster Electric Guitars @$500
> 5 Behringer X1622USB Mixers @$225
> 5 Behringer Powerplay HA8000 Headphone Amplifiers @$150
> 20 Yamaha RH2C Headphones @$30
> 20 Shure SM58 microphones w/stands @$120
> Peavey Triflex II Portable Sound System $900
> Cables and miscellaneous $1000
> Approximate Total (without any educational discount) $15,000
> (Selmer Model 41 Contra Bass Clarinet, approximately $24,000)

4   Libby Larson's NASM speech (referenced also in Chapter 4) is a very interesting discussion concerning acoustic and produced sound. See the full text of Libby Larson's NASM speech at: http://libbylarsen.com/as_the-role-of-the-musician.

Readings and References

Deci, E. L. and Ryan, R. M. (eds.) (2002). *Handbook of Self-Determination Research.* Rochester, NY: University of Rochester Press.

Green, L. (2008). *Music, Informal Learning and the School: A New Classroom Pedagogy.* Surrey, England: Ashgate.

6 Closing Thoughts

You are a part of a professional organization. Teaching music in the schools is more than a job. The music education profession in the United States has a long and distinguished history of practice, and is quickly developing a robust research component. We have taken group performance to amazing levels and our ensembles have been a prominent part of the secondary school experience. But as we move further into the twenty-first century the winds of change have become a storm. The world has changed and continues to change at an increasingly faster rate. Our profession, on the other hand, has made every attempt possible to avoid change. We continue to do things the way we did them at the start of the twentieth century, assuming if it worked then it should work now. We have become very good at making excuses to explain enrollment problems and other woes, figuring it all must be someone else's fault.

Have you seen racehorses wearing blinders? I think they are normally referred to as blinkers, and they prevent the horse from seeing to the rear, and sometimes to the sides. The intent is to keep the horse focused on what they are doing and to help them from being distracted or spooked. It is as if the music education profession has on a set of blinkers. The blinkers keep us focused on what we are doing so we aren't distracted (or spooked) by everything else that is going on. We are so focused on, and happy with, the way we produce music, that we don't notice there are other ways to create it. It is time for us to remove our blinkers.

As I mentioned in Chapter 4, Gary McPherson and Karin Hendricks (2010) conducted an interesting research study using a sample of 3037 students in the United States as part of a larger international study. A portion of this study examined the participation interest, in and out of school, of students for music, art, PE, English, math, and science at grades six, middle school and high school. They found that outside of school, elementary and middle school student's interest for participating in music was higher than for all the other subject areas except

PE. For the high school students, interest for music participation outside school was higher than for any of the other subjects. Interest for in-school music participation, however, was the lowest-ranked subject overall with significantly lower scores than for *all the other subjects*. Let me say that again ... outside of school, students were very interested in musical participation, but inside school students were less interested in music participation than they were for participation in art, PE, English, math *and* science!

Wait! Quick! Put those blinkers back on! Seeing these data might distract us from what we do. Talk about "spooky!" Well, the truth is, seeing these data *should* distract and spook us. In their research report, McPherson and Hendricks quoted Bennett Reimer (2004) and his thoughts are most applicable here as well:

> Music is thriving in America, in its rich array of types and styles and ways to be involved that our multimusical culture makes so readily available to all. Music education is not thriving comparably. We have tended to hunker down with our narrow preferences and limited opportunities and then, because we are dangerously irrelevant, we advocate, advocate, advocate – not for fundamental change in music education but for unquestioning support for what we have traditionally chosen to offer. We must advocate so furiously because we are selling what few care to buy. No wonder we are so unpersuasive and have to sell harder and harder. Our most urgent task, our way out of our unreality, is to more fully satisfy the actual musical needs and enthusiasms so plentiful all around us while adding to people's musical satisfactions the breadth and depth we are professionally qualified to help them achieve.
>
> (Reimer 2004, p. 34)

The "way out of our unreality," is to remove our blinkers once and for all. We must stop focusing solely on what we have been doing, and begin to take in all the possibilities. It is time to make the term "music in the schools" mean something more than musical groups based on a nineteenth-century model. It is time to focus more on student needs than our needs. It is time, once again, to make music education in the United States relevant within the society we live. Removing the blinkers is a big bold step. Making change a reality in the profession is an even bigger step. As the future of music education, you are the hope for our profession. You have the opportunity to create a different paradigm in music education.

Amazing societal changes have brought us to where we are today. These changes keep on coming. Amazing changes in music making have also brought us to where we are today. These changes keep on coming as well. There are two ways to approach change. One is through fear, the other through excitement. It is our choice. It is your choice. I suggest to you that the future of the music education profession is bright and full of exciting possibilities. There is a lot of work to be done, but we should take great delight in this work as we create new and exhilarating models of music education. If you hadn't already removed your blinkers, I hope this book may have helped you take that step. With our eyes wide open we can make music education truly meaningful and relevant once again.

Readings and References

McPherson, G. E. and Hendricks, K. S. (2010). Students' motivation to study music: The United States of America. *Research Studies in Music Education* 32(2): 201–213.

Reimer, B. (2004). Reconceiving the standards and the school music program. *Music Educators Journal* 91(1): 33–37.

Index